Promises of *Hope* for Difficult Times

Jane Kirkpatrick

HARVEST HOUSE PUBLISHERS™
EUGENE, OREGON

Cover design by Koechel Peterson & Associates, Inc., Minneapolis, Minnesota

Cover photo © Hemera/ Thinkstock

Published in association with Hartline Literary Agency, LLC of 123 Queenston Drive, Pittsburgh, PA 15235

PROMISES OF HOPE FOR DIFFICULT TIMES

Copyright © 2013 by Jane Kirkpatrick
Published by Harvest House Publishers
Eugene, Oregon 97402
www.harvesthousepublishers.com

ISBN 978-0-7369-4994-1 (pbk.)
ISBN 978-0-7369-4996-5 (eBook)

Printed in China

13 14 15 16 17 18 19 20 21 22 / RDS-CD / 10 9 8 7 6 5 4 3 2 1

To Jerry
and to the Caregiver Support Group of
First Presbyterian Church in Bend, Oregon.
All helped me through the difficult times.

Acknowledgments

*With gratitude to Rod Morris, my editor;
the team at Harvest House Publishers;
my agent, Joyce Hart, and those who
shared their stories of care.*

A Word to the Reader

he nineteenth-century poet, Rainer Maria Rilke, wrote, "I describe myself as a landscape studied at length and in detail...or like a word I am coming to understand." I find nurture from the landscapes of the high desert where I live and at the sea where we vacation and even in the concrete forests of large cities where I often work. I discover things I believe God wants me to consider when I am present in those places and take time to consider God's Word, if only for a few moments a day.

These words I've written for you arose from a variety of landscapes while my husband and I experienced changes in health, family constellation, and grief over leaving a place we'd carved out of hostile landscape and lived on for more than a quarter century. Many of those transitions were difficult, yet always we found the promise of hope that thrived within the turmoil. This devotional is a result of writing of that hope and the insights gained during those difficult days.

It's my hope that this little book will bring you into a quiet place where Scripture and another's "coming to understand" might bring you nurture. You may choose to read the Scripture passage from your Bible and to read verses before and after for more context and to allow time for God to speak to you.

Don't feel you have to read the book straight through or even every day. Select a verse and words and let them invite you to receive the hope placed within. Never hesitate to write in the margins where God's insights can bring you back to the wisdom of Scripture. Be encouraged to read, pause, contemplate, and find respite as you let the words bring you understanding and hope for the difficult times you're facing.

Warmly,

Jane Kirkpatrick

Is not wisdom found among the aged?
Does not long life bring understanding?

Job 12:12

Jerry and I drove back to the ranch, a place we'd lived for twenty-six years. It's a remote acreage along a wild and scenic river, down a serpentine road with dips and curves that become essentially a one-lane dirt road. We lived seven miles from the mailbox and eleven miles from pavement. Because with age came wisdom, we recently left for health reasons and because another winter loomed daunting in our minds.

Going back after six months away, we cried a bit for what had been. Not a sadness really but a remembering. Building a life on Starvation Lane was a grand adventure that shaped us and many others. Neither of us wishes we had not made that trek to dream and build and make a way beside that river. But neither do we regret the move we made to leave it behind. This is a good place to be in one's life: happy for past choices; happy for present ones.

It was those years on that ranch where I learned to trust that if I needed to leave, the road would be passable. Somehow, bills would get paid. We'd recover from accidents we didn't prevent. I learned there to take deep breaths and not to wonder what the future held but to instead cherish what there was.

The futon folded out the night we returned for a visit. It was a fine bed for us. The pellet stove started right up, which was good as the night wore cool, black, and still. Not even coyotes howled. Only the hum of the refrigerator lulled us asleep.

In the morning we reminded each other of what God had done for us in that place and how we'd been blessed now with a new home closer to hospitals and services we had greater need for. We closed the gate and sighed.

We're home now, surrounded with memories not meant to hold us hostage but to transform. Even as we age, we can change, make a new way, drive down new roads and find blessings wherever we're allowed to bloom. Our journey back reminds us.

*A word fitly spoken
is like apples of gold in a setting of silver.*

Proverbs 25:11 (NRSV)

Our words often trip past each other and stumble us on our journey. Since his stroke, my husband's speech comes labored, and he sometimes neglects to put all the words into the sentence. I rush ahead and think I know what Jerry's going to say, but I'm often wrong. For someone who lives with words, works with words, this confusion of meaning with someone I care about is frustrating.

"My words cannot suffice to my heart," wrote Saint Augustine centuries ago, and it's how I feel when misunderstandings cloud the day already filled with challenge.

"It is a spiritual discipline to find the right word to set down next to another word in a way that reaches across boundaries and distances," wrote Stephanie Paulsell, who teaches the practice of ministry at Harvard Divinity School. "Haunting every word is the presence of the word God spoke to reach out to us. In a culture in which words are flung out not as lifelines but as invective, it is an act of resistance to measure our words against the reconciling work of the Word that gives life and hope."

Today, at least once, I will pause before assuming I know what someone I love means and let the reconciling work of the Word grant life and hope.

*Show me your ways, LORD, teach me
your paths. Guide me in your truth and
teach me, for you are God my Savior,
and my hope is in you all day long.*

Psalm 25:4-5

I'm making up to-do lists: doctor appointments; medication pickup; remember the blood pressure/weight/heart rate list to share with the cardio rehab people.

Often in my presentations about writing, I talk about a Harvard study where people with asthma and arthritis were asked to spend twenty minutes, three times a week writing down their stories. Who was driving them crazy, what committee they'd never work on again, how they spent the morning with their best friend. They didn't have to show their words to anyone or come to any conclusions. A control group spent the same amount of time, but their writing consisted of to-do lists.

At the end of the trial period, there was a clinically significant reduction in the amount of pain medication needed and the number of asthmatic attacks for the people who told themselves their stories. For the to-do list people? Absolutely no change. I've always said those list people might have lied because when I look at my to-do list, I want more pain medication.

Better than all those lists would be to pause and be taught, to note how I'm feeling this day, to tell my story and witness to how God is intersecting in my life, pulling me closer, opening my heart on days of drain. A short note will do. Lists of things for which I'm grateful. Struggles I write down and then give to God. No need to show it to anyone else.

Hope swirls within the words I write.

Gracious words are a honeycomb,
sweet to the soul and healing to the bones.

Proverbs 16:24

Much of my writing is wrapped in exploring historical women's lives. I seek to discover where these women drew their strength from. Did they stand alone, strong as bone? How did they mend when they felt broken? What gave them strength to cross the bridge of a woman's life, moving from hungering child to giving mother to caring daughter or wife to become that strong woman? What can they show us for our own time of challenge?

I once asked a group of second graders what the word *powerful* meant to them. One said, "Big and strong like on the playground." Another suggested, "Rich. Powerful means lots of money." They speculated back and forth. But one young boy in the front row took my breath away when he said, "Oh no. Powerful is when you want to quit but you keep going."

I cherish that child's wisdom especially on days when I want to quit. When the chaos seems too much; when the uncertainty drains my goodwill; when laughter is a distant memory and the treasured times of closeness threaten to disappear forever. I think of those historical women who tended others without benefit of medications or close neighbors for support. They often tended children, too, and planted and harvested crops, chopped wood for the winter. How often did they want to quit? But they kept going. Perhaps it was a pleasant word from another in a letter that encouraged. Maybe a child's wise comment or an unexpected neighbor's stopping by with words of support.

James reminds us to consider it joy to face trials and that such testing builds perseverance and perseverance must "finish its work" so that we may be mature and complete (James 1:2-4). Take in the gracious or pleasant words of children, and if these are missing in our days, we can speak kind words to ourselves. We can repeat the promises of Scripture.

We are made powerful. We are created to be persevering. We bring health to our bones.

Sow your seed in the morning, and at evening
let your hands not be idle, for you do not
know which will succeed, whether this or
that, or whether both will do equally well.

Ecclesiastes 11:6

The flower beds were overgrown with grass and leggy weeds. Somehow, while we were busy tending to the latest crisis, grass and greens shoved through the lupine and tiger lilies covering the borders, choking out flowering things.

"How could the beds have gotten so overgrown in such a short time?" I asked my husband.

"It doesn't take much neglect for things to begin to deteriorate," he answered.

On the list of things to be done, weeding flower beds placed close to the bottom. A friend said to pull weeds only until it wasn't fun anymore, then do something else. But even that pacing failed to ease the growing jungle that began to resemble our lives: overgrown; confused borders between work and worry with no play built in at all; difficulty finding the blooms in the midst of the weeds; neglect threatening to deteriorate relationships that mattered.

I needed help. And so I asked for it, one of the hardest things to do in times of peril.

When the workers left after spending the day, I could

not believe how my spirit lifted! The beds were edged again, with a clean border I could see. Someone who knew weeds from flowers had given new life to the foliage the previous owners planted. Those plants would flourish now, no longer choked by fast-growing grass. Some well-placed ground cover, biodegradable additives to retard the weeds, and my pulling errant grasses every day promised flower beds that bring nurture rather than reminders of what we hadn't done.

I look out at those beds and now see joy—something not to neglect finding in times of trial—and the respite of tiger lilies reminding me of God's presence among the weeds.

"Consider how the wild flowers grow."

Luke 12:27

oday I am grateful for the little things. A washing machine and clothes dryer that work. A garage with room for a vehicle and not just storage. Dogs that are healthy and friendly. Neighbors who stay connected but aren't intrusive. The view out my window of wild flowers surrounding a labyrinth for contemplative prayer. The ability to pay the phone and electric bill when they're due.

Reminding myself of those thing the faucet breaks and water pours ov or the car won't start because of a dead get cheatgrass in their ears and have narian to remove it. I've even taken to things I'm grateful for, a list to help m tle tragedies threaten to become large dies we're already dealing with.

This morning, in the desert area of the yard, bloom five sego lilies. They bloom following long harsh winters and don't bloom every year. Their beauty reminds me that out of tragedy can come beauty and hope as God walks with us.

"Be patient with me."
Matthew 18:26,29

*I*t's been a difficult week. I was hospitalized with ulcers—eight of them! These are not the kind caused by a bacteria and easily treated with antibiotics but rather from the use of pain relievers and likely…from stress.

As someone steeped in mental health treatment, the idea that stress has found its way into damaging my body is, well, humiliating. The *shoulds* come out to shout. I should know how to manage stress. I should take better care of myself. I should be able to handle the tensions of our lives without physical damage. My greatest *should* was that as a caregiver, I should be home, taking care of my husband instead of him watering plants, feeding the dogs, and visiting me at the hospital. But *shoulds* are weights meant to be tossed off.

This verse—"Be patient with me"—wrapped within a story of forgiveness (Matthew 18:21-35), jumped out at me. At first I made it another *should*—I should be more patient. But then I saw it as a prayer just as the slave who owed the debt sought more time and forgiveness for being behind.

Today I seek that patience, too, with the hope that as God grants it, I can receive it and be gracious, forgiving myself and granting patience to those around me. It's a reminder that I am human, in need of patience, a word that is old and means "endurance with calmness," especially for one under medical treatment.

God grant me endurance and calmness this day.

*The angel of the LORD encamps around
those who fear him, and he delivers them.*

Psalm 34:7

My twenty-five-year-old nephew headed off today to new adventures—seeking a job across the continent, driving a car stocked with clothes and computer and things to bring him comfort when he arrives in California. Another young friend, recently graduated, cleans houses while living again with her parents because it's the job she can do while putting in her applications for work related to her degree. A granddaughter has her first job far from home and right now suffers with flu.

Their parents agonize, wanting them to be launched and yet missing them already; wanting them to find their place in this world and hoping they've given them the tools, yet wishing they were close enough to bring them hot soup and a healing touch. Their children's dreams are half finished. They aren't where they will one day be, but they are also not where they've been. Yet in that uncertainty they can't sit down and contemplate; they have to keep moving, telling themselves that they aren't where they'll one day be, things will change, it will get better.

Those of us who love these young adventurers can be assured that they are not alone in that uncertain place. I pray for angels to encamp around them, to keep them safe. I remind myself that God is even now working out the next step on their paths. Those young adults can be buoyed along by the prayers of their families, trusting that the ups and downs of this challenging trail will help to shape them, prepare them for when they arrive at the place they're called to be. It is the best we can give them as they launch…and it serves to remind me that God provides the cover and God delivers.

"Never will I leave you;
never will I forsake you."

Hebrews 13:5

The empty nest. That's what my friend calls it having sent her only child off to college. Familiar routines and sounds, the scent of her son's shampoo, are all gone now. Though she goes to work each day as she always did, fixes meals for her husband, and reads the Sunday paper after church and watches the Seahawks play, as is their pattern, nothing seems right. An important participant is missing—a child who has left the nest.

On our ranch in the spring we would often hear the noises of the Canada geese that had nested in the rimrocks as they sent their goslings out of the nests. As they honked and howled, we'd watch through binoculars this ritual of parenting, this setting aside of any reservations to make sure the offspring encounter the next test of time and leave despite the protest. I think of my friend as I watch those birds do what is part of their nature.

My friend and her husband prepared the way so their son could leave. He had the confidence to withstand new trials because his parents gave him wisdom and experience and helped him through those smaller challenges that prepared him for the larger ones: how to solve a problem on his own; how to reconcile a troubled relationship; how to make a change without a lot of friction.

Perhaps most of all, my friend swallowed her pain

knowing that through her prayers her son does not go alone. Her nest will one day be filled with other treasures: a visit home from her son with a load of laundry in tow; perhaps more time for guests or ministry as the child's room changes to include a writing space, a quilting spot, a reading room.

The changes define nesting. Through it all we are reminded: "Never will I leave you; never will I forsake you." That message rings true for the child sent on to the next step of his life and for the one at home still nesting.

Perfect love drives out fear.

1 John 4:18

My husband has bouts of vertigo. There are medical explanations for this discombobulating experience when the world seems to spin. His balance is that of a man with one leg still asleep as he tries to take a step. For me, who tries to walk beside him, the medical cause is less troubling than the fears: What if he falls and I can't get him up? What if he breaks a hip? What if he never recovers from this? What if he stumbles on me and we both are injured?

I'm very creative when it comes to fears.

Someone once told me that the letters in the word *fear* stand for *false evidence appearing real.* It is that practice we have of projecting things into the future, of not living in the moment, that brings on fear. Instead of thinking my husband should lie down where he is and complete the Epley maneuver (a series of movements to relieve vertigo), my mind races to the worst case scenario, and I pull out the bedpan of fear.

Perfect love, Scripture tells us, casts out all fear. There is no false evidence in God's promises to be there for this moment and to be with us through the next. As Brian McClaren in his book *Naked Spirituality* reminds us, *being here* is a beginning of a deeper relationship with God. I need to keep my thoughts in this moment today, not rush into the future.

*The LORD sustains them on their sickbed
and restores them from their bed of illness.*

Psalm 41:3

The house next door has been empty all the while we've lived here, over a year now. A neighbor stays in touch with the people who lost their home when the woman was let go from her job of nineteen years and the husband was injured. The neighbor remains connected even though the people have moved out of the area. I learned that the wife now suffers from a terminal illness as well. There's new interest in someone buying the house, and the neighbor tells me the woman hopes to get this house sale resolved so her family won't have that worry along with the ache of a loved one's illness and likely death.

I don't know this woman or her family, but I feel sadness for her and all the others who find themselves lost in the world of chaos oozed out from illness and injury. I remind myself that uncertainty is very much what living looks like. Sometimes it may be financial uncertainty; other times it's a relationship that causes us to wonder if we will ever have a steady course of predictability. Theologian Paul Tillich reminds us that living with uncertainty is one of the tasks of being human, but I rail against its familiarity.

So when I begin to obsess about those things I have no control over, I remind myself of the two things I can always control and I focus on them: being clear about what matters in my life and having the courage to act on that. The restoration promised in the psalm may not be in this life. But until then, I will draw on the promise to gain strength to pray for those in peril and to remember what matters for today: to be present to the ones I care deeply about and, for just a moment, to set aside the uncertainty and chaos and claim the promise of the psalm and thus be sustained.

A psalm. For giving grateful praise.

Psalm 100

Someone pointed out that Psalm 100 is rich with verbs: *Shout. Worship. Come. Enter. Give.* Verbs are action words and they bring energy and description to a piece, more than adjectives or adverbs. *Love* is a verb too, and it's been my experience that sometimes it's the action of love that speaks louder than the emotion.

A friend of mine cares for her husband who is dying of brain cancer. She lives with the weight of such verbs as: changing his night diaper; cleaning sheets and bedpans; freshening his water; reminding him to swallow; setting aside the tasks necessary for their livelihood. On this day she writes that the hospice worker says he has "turned the corner," and she knows that he no longer is "living with brain cancer" but rather "dying of brain cancer." *Living* and *dying* are verbs too. Yet her journey with her husband is filled with gratitude verbs: gratitude for tending him, for ushering him from this world to the next.

To give thanks in the midst of grief is perhaps the strongest verb of all, and through it God grants us respite, peace, and assurance. Today I will draw on those verbs and remember that love is full of action.

> "He will wipe every tear from their
> eyes. There will be no more death or
> mourning or crying or pain, for the old
> order of things has passed away."
>
> *Revelation 21:4*

There are scenes. Often they occur on holidays. Christmas was a trying time of family discord; Easter carries special memories of family betrayal, disappointment, and anxiety.

Or maybe the uproar happens at a funeral that is filled with grief, and to avoid the pain, someone says something held back while the loved one lived, but now it is spoken in a way and at a time the rest of us feel is boldly inappropriate. Hearts pound, voices raise enough to scare the children, who begin to cry, and the memory of that loved one is tainted.

Afterward, even while I'm still full of indignation, I'm reminded of what is yet to be.

"He will wipe every tear."

"There will be no more death or mourning or crying or pain."

"The old order of things has passed away."

Not soon enough, I mumble. And yet out of those scenes I am reminded of the promise that this too will pass.

Today, I will cling to that. These disruptions, though painful, could transform me if I allow them and do not let the images define me, but act instead to see them as arrows to a better future.

I will praise you because I am fearfully
and wonderfully made; your works are
wonderful, I know that full well.

Psalm 139:14

It would be nice if everything went the way I planned, but it does not, and this family trial of misunderstanding over money leeches vigor from a mind and body already fatigued by tending to one I love. But my character is chiseled—as the word *charakter* in Greek implies—in the worst of times. What is left behind is who I am, and it is shaped by God's intention.

In a good novel, we want trouble for our characters, for it's through that trouble the characters are shaped, and we come to know them as distinctive and complete. But in life we'd like no trouble, just the smoothness of the marble before it's carved.

But would I want to forgo a Michelangelo just to keep the marble as a lump of smooth possibilities?

If I ask a friend to tell me of a time when she was strong, she would tell a story of a challenge that she had and how she overcame it. In this present challenge, I'm trying to remember that I am being carved out of material created by a loving God who knows what I'll become before I do. It is now when I should praise God, who keeps the promise that we are each fearfully and wonderfully made, and trust in that promise.

> *"Come off by yourselves; let's take a*
> *break and get a little rest." For there*
> *was constant coming and going.*
>
> *Mark 6:31* (MSG)

*I*t's said that the first note of every musical composition is silence. Musicians take a deep breath and breathe in the beginning of what they'll need for the coming and going of the piece.

I was once asked to speak at an event and was given the charge "inspire us." In looking up the definition of *inspiration,* I came upon "the act of breathing in." That's what we need to sustain the rhythm of our lives, taking in things we can draw upon and find inspiration. Things that fill us.

So often I forget to take that break and breathe in inspiration. Celebration days are especially troubling. Those are the times when I ought to have the greatest silence to begin my day, and instead I'm adding to the to-do list of my life. Trim the tree; purchase the Easter ham; bake the birthday cake. What ought to be a time of joy becomes a burden for simply getting things finished.

The word *celebration* means "to fill up with joy," and the definition suggests doing it over and over again. The only way to celebrate in the midst of the constant coming and going is to take that break, get a little rest, come off by myself as Jesus modeled for His disciples. Inhale so I can be inspired for the duties and allow the joys of the day to define the celebration.

*Early on a Sunday morning, as
the new day was dawning…*

Matthew 28:1 (NLT)

I remember a sermon from when I was a child where our pastor held up an empty wooden spool of thread. The label on the spool end had the company name, the color name, and the letters ONT. The letters, he noted, stood for "our new thread," and the sermon spoke of how symbols can be easily forgotten or carry little meaning over time. The company, the Clark Thread Company, had been in the business of making thread for years, and their innovative new thread was no longer new at all.

I think it was the first time I understood what a metaphor was. Or maybe I remember it because the pastor used a show-and-tell item that allowed me at the age of eight to grasp what he was telling us: to not let our faith carry a meaningless symbol.

The cross is not a mere symbol of a former time; it represents a new dawning every day. My daily Scripture readings are a reminder to make *our new thread* relevant for the challenges of each day. These are not words of the past but words meant to inspire, warm, comfort, encourage, and bless in this new day.

*Whether you turn to the right or to the
left, your ears will hear a voice behind
you, saying, "This is the way; walk in it."*

Isaiah 30:21

On my desk is a glass coaster with an inuksuk symbol cut into the center. Shaped like a human and made of square rocks piled on top of each other, the image is created by Inuit people of Canada to represent human forms that act as guideposts for people traveling the tundra. It was the logo used for the 2010 Winter Olympics held in British Columbia.

I learned later that the logo of the inuksuk held controversy as many First Americans—non-Inuit people of the north—said it was less representative of other native symbols such as totems or singular carvings of whales or birds created by great Northwest tribes. Instead of representing a guidepost for travelers, it had become a symbol of dissent.

When I set my cup of tea upon that coaster, I'm reminded of the charge to make my faith a guidepost, something I step inside of on this journey through troubled times. There may be dissent, disagreements about what it all means, but it is still a guidepost giving me direction, helping me listen for those words "This is the way; walk in it."

It's how I move through the challenging days ahead.

I do not understand what I do. For what I want to do I do not do, but what I hate I do.

Romans 7:15

Today I'm frustrated and annoyed. It takes my husband so much longer to brush his teeth, to finish his meal, to get out the words he intends to say. When we take walks, hand in hand, I feel as though I'm pulling him along instead of our walking side by side. My head knows these changes are the result of the stroke, or perhaps his getting older, and I *should* be patient and understanding. But my heart aches and my gut hurts as I tap my proverbial foot, anxious for him to pick up his feet, move along. Later, I'm filled with remorse for my lack of compassion, the rearing of my addiction to control. I fail to recognize my upset as sadness, loss, my difficulty in accepting change.

I once had a character say, "If you always do what you've always done, you'll always get what you've always gotten." And in my head, I know that if I want something to be different, I must make the change, not wait for someone else or, worse, believe that I can cause another to change and thus make my life easier.

But still I try, until the apostle Paul's words of his doing what he wishes he didn't and not doing what he intends are made contemporary. I know what I'm to do and how to do it, yet I don't. Paul's story reminds me to take a deep breath. I am human too, doing the best I can.

I didn't start out to be an impatient harpy cackling at the ones I love. I didn't intend to act like my pace in the relationship is all that matters.

God's intervening love is my only hope that I won't always do what I've always done. Instead, I'll do something different today giving my husband's words time to form, giving him my undivided attention, mindful that whatever it is I think I have to do so hurriedly—can wait.

I lift up my eyes to the mountains—
where does my help come from?

Psalm 121:1

focused on the keyboard, the only light in the room coming from the computer screen. A deadline loomed, so even though we had taken time to vacation in sunny southern Baja Mexico, I had work to do. I could hardly call it work; it gave me joy to find a way to tell the stories that encouraged people and celebrated the lives of historical persons, especially women. My eyes would open around 5:00 a.m., and after morning prayers, I'd rise and go into the darkened living room to write, putting in two to three hours before the rest of the day began.

I wrote, as steeped in story as in prayer.

An hour or two passed, and then for some reason, I lifted my eyes to discover that the room had gotten lighter. I turned toward the Sea of Cortez. Magenta streaked the skies speared by palm trees waving in the morning wind. Even the water was a sea of pink bordered by white foam that brushed the sandy shore. Tiny lights from the hotel compound still flickered, not yet realizing they could not compete with the brilliance of the sunrise nor were they needed now, the natural light a gift from God.

I almost missed that moment of beauty. So focused on both joy and obligation, I might not have raised my eyes. Yet something moved me from the screen to take in that view that caused me to experience awe.

Surely God wants us to be focused on more than the task at hand, the purposes He gives us, on trusting Him through difficult times. There are higher things, and the momentary brilliance of a sunrise is surely worthy of my focus, my hearth-heart, my passion. From it I have the memory, a reminder that God's gifts are everywhere, and it pleases Him that I take the time to receive them.

He rained down manna for the people to eat,
he gave them the grain of heaven.

Psalm 78:24

My father had died a few months earlier; my mom was in an assisted living facility two hours from our remote ranch. I'd recently left my day job after seventeen years, hoping our ranch and my writing would be enough to sustain us. Once again we were stepping out on a cloud of faith believing we wouldn't fall through. Then my stepson and his wife had legal troubles, and we decided to take in our fifteen-year-old granddaughter.

The question that kept coming to me in my morning hour of quiet wasn't "Why?" but "Will we be enough?" Will we have the stamina to deal with the needs of a teenager? Will we be able to get her to school twenty-five miles away each day and back? Will our love for her and her parents, too, be sufficient to help us all heal from the choices they'd made? Will the finances stretch to meet everyone's needs?

I thought of the Israelites fleeing Egypt and how they worried about their future. God gave them *manna,* a word that in Hebrew translates as "What is it?" What it was proved to be just enough each day to get them through. Nothing overflowing but sufficient to sustain them, enough to remind them to have faith even in the wilderness.

At a women's retreat a few weeks after our granddaughter's arrival, I asked the group of women to form a circle and find a partner. "Tell your partner something you will take home from this retreat that will help remind you of God's presence in your life," I suggested. Because we had an uneven number, I also had to be in the circle to make it complete. My mind had been focused on these women and this retreat, but as we prepared to go home, the worm of worry began to slither into my thoughts.

"Look at your partner and see them as Jesus might: with loving eyes. Ask God to give you a word they can take with them to help sustain them as they return home."

The woman across from me looked into my eyes with such warmth. "Enough," she said. "That's the word that comes to me. You will be enough; God will be enough." I felt tears on my cheeks. "It's just a little word," she added almost apologetically, touching my hand with comfort.

"Yes, a little word given at my great moment of need," I said. "Thank you for listening to God's heart and giving me that manna."

The very word that had haunted me these past weeks of disruption and turmoil had been given as sustenance—not as a question but as an answer. I just needed to remember daily to pick it up and savor it. I might not be enough—but God would provide.

And so God does.

The Holy Spirit said to Philip,
"Go over and walk along beside…"

Acts 8:29 NLT

He had that Floridian tan and oil-black hair, and he had already donned the headphones before he sank into the aisle seat next to me. I slept the first hour or so after takeoff out of Orlando heading to Denver, and when I woke, I saw that the man next to me watched Christmas video scenes on his iPhone, headphones still intact.

I read. We didn't speak.

Somewhere over the Great Plains I noticed his shoulders begin to shake, and despite the airplane noise I could hear him choking back sobs and then, unable to, his muffled cries. His agony reached across to me, and while I sent him thoughts of comfort, it didn't seem enough. When he left to go to the restroom, I told Jerry of the sadness I'd witnessed.

"I should say something," I said.

"But what?" Jerry answered.

Yes, *but what?*

Would saying anything be intrusive? He'd obviously tried to hide his tearful sobs and he'd made no eye contact with me, had said nothing during the two hours we'd sat beside each other cocooned in the airplane's capsule. I brooded, torn between allowing privacy for pain and yet a belief in connection, in reaching out, that shared burdens are made lighter.

He returned, replaced his headphones.

I decided to take a risk. I touched his shoulder, pressing enough for him to know it wasn't just an unintended brush against him. He startled and removed his headphones, leaned away as he looked at me.

"I hope within your sadness," I said, "that you have someone to walk beside you."

He stared at me for a moment and then, his shoulders sinking, said, "Thank you. Thank you." He reached out his hand and introduced himself, and then began to tell his story, how he had just spent Christmas with his extended family whom he hadn't seen in seventeen years.

"It was overwhelming," he said. "The tears were not only of sadness, for what I'd missed by being out of touch, but for joy too. I wasn't sure how I'd be received. I was just going to arrive, say hello, maybe have a meal with them, then leave. But I stayed, even missed my flight, so I got on this one instead. I…I'm Hispanic, but learned my family has German roots too, and I saw photographs of ancestors for the first time and heard their stories of all they'd endured for their families, of what always mattered to them—family. It's all that matters," he said, "knowing that there are those who love you and who will embrace you."

"It's good you let them in," I said.

He paused. "Yes. Yes it is."

We talked awhile longer, until the plane landed in fact, and then he said, "Thank you for reaching out to me. I tried not to be obvious. I was just overcome with emotion." I nodded. Then he added, "When you said you hoped there was someone to walk beside me in my sadness, what did you mean? A friend, a spirit?"

"All of that," I said.

"Well, I have God to walk beside me. But I thank you for reminding me."

I'll likely never see this man again. And while he thinks that I touched him in some way, he touched me too. I can get so caught up in the vagaries of every day—the news, the trials that I think I face—and often forget the very foundations of what sustains me. I have someone to walk beside me too—friends, God—if only I allow.

Your eyes saw my unformed body; all the days ordained for me were written in your book before one of them came to be.

Psalm 139:16

We've talked often of mortality. With Jerry's many health challenges through the years—eleven broken vertebra giving chronic pain, cancer, a perforated colon, stroke, and heart attack (among others)—and with him being sixteen years older than me, we often speak as though he will go first. Yet who can know?

I know we are all dying, wasting away from the moment we arrive, shedding off cells of skin, wearing down all that was fearfully and wonderfully made while still plunging forward, often acting as though we will never die. I know from Psalm 139 that all our days are in God's hands. Yet my heart carries worry like hot water in a teacup while crossing a roaring stream. That which is worrisome is contained inside the crucible of God's creation, and even if the hot water spills, it will disappear inside the stream I'm standing in, a mere nothing in the scheme of things. I know this in my head, but my heart resists accepting the nature of what is.

For today I will imagine drinking the hot water in the teacup, letting it quench my thirst as only water can. I will acknowledge that I'm in that roaring stream, but so far my legs have held me up against the water's force. I can take another step, which is all that is required. And I have a companion walking beside me. For the moment it is Jerry, but tomorrow it may be a friend or, as I near the shore, it may be only Jesus reminding me to look ahead to the green pastures on the other side.

When they could not find a way…
they went up on the roof and lowered him on
his mat through the tiles…right in front of Jesus.

Luke 5:19

Today I attended my first caregiver's support group, a mountain of reluctance overcome. That resistance came from questions such as, who am I to *need* the help of others? I'm a counselor myself. I write books that celebrate healing. My husband's health needs are minor compared to so many. My husband continues to be quite capable, so why do I think I need support?

Jerry's comment the week before spurred me forward. While we walked the beach of San Jose del Cabo, he said, "You seem so far away. I feel like I've lost my best friend." His words were similar to ones I told myself shortly after his stroke: *so far away, my best friend gone.* But in time I'd expressed that loss to him, and slowly, as he exercised, followed the doctor's orders, he began to come back, the vacant look in his eyes wisping away. Friends sent me information on strokes, and others set me up with a stroke magazine giving monthly encouragement as well as information. But all was different now; some things never returned.

I became less of a friend and more of a hoverer. Our interactions were around doctor appointments, had he taken his medication, trying to find things he'd put away but now couldn't remember where. The long pauses between sentences and the difficulty of his sometimes slurred words brought frustration rather than understanding. How would I take care of him if he got worse? What about the future should something happen to prevent my being able to care for him or to cause me to need care?

Anxiety and, yes, resentment grew. I began to see him not as my partner and friend but as my sister I helped care for in her dying or my father in his dementia or my mom with her congestive heart condition. I loved them all through their dying, but they were not my husband, and they had many caregivers besides just me.

At church on Sunday we sat next to the care coordinator for the caregiver support group. I do not believe in coincidences. "I need to join your group," I heard myself say. "It's time?" she answered, as though she understood that journey where one day we might feel strong enough and another day know we need friends to bring us closer to healing.

The man being lowered through the roof of the house where Jesus healed speaks to that journey of reaching out. Friends will often know what must be done to bring about healing even when the action may seem preposterous—lowering someone through a roof? But the sick man's friends saw his need and together they brought the man to Jesus. That's what friends are for, and our work as friends and caregivers is to receive the gift friends are willing to give.

*"See how the flowers of the field
grow. They do not labor or spin."*

Matthew 6:28

A winter sign outside Old South Church in Boston reads: "The garden is also a proclamation of our faith, that beauty will spring from barrenness and form out of chaos, life out of death. Here in the coldest and darkest time we make bold to proclaim that spring and life are on their way."

Hulda Klager, a German immigrant living in the early 1900s in Washington State, was passionate about her garden and the propagation of lilacs. Because of where her family lived at the confluence of two great rivers, her garden was often flooded. If she had time, she'd pull her lilacs and float the plants on rafts tied to trees in her yard, watching them bob while she waited for the water to recede. After the flood, she would begin again. Her persistence and constant faith that life would spring from death has become a promise to remember in my own life.

Memory and faith are the garden tools that will bring form out of chaos. Whatever is at this moment—the sadness or barrenness, dark or cold—is temporary. New life awaits.

It is the promise of spring.

*And the disciples picked up twelve
basketfuls of broken pieces.*

Mark 6:43

In 1812 in Boston, a sewing circle formed named the Fragment Society. They began their work that lasted nearly two hundred years providing clothing for children and layettes for newborns. Their hope was to meet the needs of those who were society's fragments, broken pieces, what was left behind after the serving of the masses.

There are days when I feel like a fragment needing threads to mend the holes that threaten to shatter like silk. Disappointment in myself, my lost temper, my resentment of what is—all threaten to tear what at times is a very fragile grasp on compassion, both for the person I'm caring for and myself.

Yet I am comforted by the story of loaves and fishes and the very idea that after all were fed, there were broken pieces left over, and Jesus did not want those left behind. Perhaps the disciples took those fragments with them; perhaps they distributed them to others they met along the way. What mattered was that even the broken pieces nurtured.

I will savor that image on my fragment days and pray that those I care for see how they nurture and trust they are not left behind.

For the word of God is alive and active…
it judges the thoughts and attitudes of the heart.

Hebrew 4:12

hey are only feelings: frustration, disappointment, anger. But feelings need not define us. We can change how we feel.

Can we, you ask? Remember that first date or maybe the class reunion when our feelings of anticipation and anxiety competed for attention? Yet after we arrived, the event began and most of us found a way to participate and to set aside at least some of those feelings. No parents ever start out saying they think they'll be a terrible parent; we all want the joy of doing well in that most important role where feelings can sometimes get the best of us.

At the caregiver group someone commented that these negative feelings we harbor can be changed…with thoughts. I know this. I believe this. But sometimes I forget.

"As I am, so I see," wrote Ralph Waldo Emerson years ago. "The real journey of discovery is not in seeking new landscapes but in seeing with new eyes" wrote French poet Marcel Proust. Each gave paths to changing how we feel by changing the way we think.

Paul's words in Hebrews grant not just the paths but the destination: God's Word, alive and active in our everyday lives, judges "the thoughts and attitudes of the heart." When I feel despairing that my situation will never change, God's voice nudges me to think, *nothing stays the same, for I make all things new.* When a sense of duty rather than compassion brings resentment, God's Word reminds me that He knows the intents of my heart. His love will bring change, if I allow. The truth of His love is there in the thoughts even on the days I do not feel it.

As for us who are strong, our duty is to bear
with the weaknesses of those who are not
strong, and not seek our own pleasure.

Romans 15:1 (WEY)

find the word *duty* intriguing. It means *responsibility* or a *job*. But it can also mean *tax* or *payment*. I have come to think of duties during struggling times as odious tasks, trials, or weights, and yet there are duties that must be done. Prescriptions need refilling, bills need paying. In some households it means getting kids up and off to school or sending resumes out and girding oneself for yet another rejection while hoping for that job or promotion. We've made commitments to our church or organizations that once filled us up but now chafe on us like a stone in our shoe.

Duty can keep us from the intimacy God wants for us. Obligation can keep me occupied but not nourished.

When there are duties in the care of others, we especially need to recognize our weakness and turn to those who are stronger than we are for the moment. Let them help us. Accept their gift of time and energy. Let them be the stake to bolster our loved ones against the present wind.

Be the weak and seek pleasure in God's love. Tomorrow we can be strong again and meet our duty having had respite through the loving hands of giving friends.

"Hear, LORD, and be merciful to me; LORD, be my help." You turned my wailing into dancing; you removed my sackcloth and clothed me with joy, that my heart may sing your praises and not be silent. LORD my God, I will praise you forever.

Psalm 30:10-12

So many of my morning prayers are laced with asking for help. *Help me be patient. Help me solve this problem. Help me be aware of You this day, of my family's needs, of opportunities to share Your love.* I pray for help to heal my wounds, to fill the cracks in my life. God answers, and I'm so busy still asking for help that I don't even notice! I need to ask for help in *receiving* the dancing or *celebrating* being clothed with joy.

A practice I've begun is to begin my quiet time with a prayer of receiving, that as I reflect on yesterday, I might name those moments perhaps quickly passed over that in reflection I can see God within. The delivery man making eye contact and asking how my day was going, using words and gestures that spoke of actual caring. The card left by a neighbor thanking us for the warm visit we'd made to see her a few days before. An unexpected check arriving at an opportune time. My remembering a nephew's birthday enough in advance to send him a card, then finding the perfect card at the post office while waiting in line. "Not everything that counts can be counted and not everything that can be counted, counts" reads the card, with credit for that wisdom given to physicist Albert Einstein.

In reflection, I see those words and the psalmist's reminder to receive what counts that I might dance with joy at God's graciousness.

"Give back to Caesar what is Caesar's…"

Mark 12:17

I call it Bounty Counting, that time of the year when taxes fall due. I fix tea, put on soft music, and then pull out the folders and forms that are the financial accounting for our past year. How did the money come in and go out more quickly than a squirrel spinning off a bird feeder? I'm not certain.

But as I fill in the blanks, look over check statements, I'm reminded of the choices we made all year long, about how we spent or invested the resources God provided. Instead of lamenting the taxes I'm now asked to pay, I'm reminded that my taxes go to help those I could not help alone.

A year when we had custody of a grandchild, I imagined my taxes going to help pay for her social worker. One spring when the county put needed gravel onto the road reaching our ranch, I imagined the check I wrote to pay our taxes assisting in road repair, not just for us but in other parts of the community. Some of our taxes paid for a new library, made the ambulance and EMTs available when Jerry had his stroke, helped put out a neighbor's fire, educated great-nieces, bought equipment for soldiers and my nephew, a policeman.

This time of year, I'm reminded that I would not be asked to give so much back if I hadn't already received so much in the first place. That attitude of gratitude reduces

the acid in my stomach, and I meet a scriptural direction
to give to Caesar what is his with the prayer that Caesar
will do good work with it, work I cannot do alone.

I finish the tea, write the check, stamp the envelope,
and take in the bounty of my day.

*Someone in the crowd said to him, "Teacher,
tell my brother to divide the inheritance
with me." Jesus replied, "Man, who
appointed me a judge or an arbiter between
you?…Watch out! Be on your guard
against all kinds of greed; life does not
consist in an abundance of possessions."*

Luke 12:15

It began fifteen years ago with my sister's divorce followed within weeks by her death. Inheritance issues. Father against sons. Aunts and uncles seeking fairness. Properties divided. Attorneys on speed dial. Money spent that might have gone for God's work. A shortened breath whenever "the dispute" comes to mind. Prayers for resolution to preserve the family seem to go unheeded.

Why did Jesus choose not to deal with the man's dispute with his brother and instead went on to tell the story of a rich farmer who continued to get richer, then worried over where to house his wealth? The story did not have a happy ending, but the epilogue was hopeful: our lives will be abundant when we are rich toward God.

This day, the long dispute will take on less weight as I step back and pray for the disputers instead of for resolution and ask not that Jesus be the arbiter but that hearts will turn to God and God's abundance.

I pray my heart goes there as well.

There is a time for everything, and a season for every activity under the heavens.

Ecclesiastes 3:1

A subtle change today. Jerry came into my office hurting more than usual. He doesn't complain much, but I can see the pain in the lines of his face. Is his back beginning to bend like the top of a shepherd's crook? He rarely comes into my office while I'm working.

"What can I do for you?" "Nothing," he says. There's no smile, no pat on my shoulder while my fingers rest on the computer keys. "Would it help to take a walk with the dogs?" I suggest. "We could do that earlier today." I'm in the middle of a project and don't really want to make that change, but I offer.

He shakes his head no. He's hurting too much. "I just wanted to see how you were doing."

I have to quell the growing anxiety within me. Annoyance and then guilt grows that I would feel interrupted by someone I love who is in pain. Worse, I begin to rush into the future. *Does his coming into the office seeking comfort mark a new deterioration? Does it mean he won't be able to take walks again? Is this what our lives will be like now? Should I get up earlier so I can do my work while he's asleep?* I know that how I respond will change him in yet other subtle ways.

I quell the annoyance, put the guilt aside. I reach for his hand. "Let me finish this section and see if you're up to that walk." He nods and turns away but still holds my palm in his. Grace connects us. It comes in the form of human touch, holding on.

"No, wait," I say. "I can finish this later. Let's go now. The sun is out." He nods. There's still no smile, no light in his eyes that pain has lessened, but he holds my hand still.

The dogs jump happily at the sight of their leashes and of him slowly putting his coat on. "This will be good," he says. And so I hope his words of truth will carry us on this walk. There is a time for my project. It can wait; this moment of grace can't.

Anyone who meets a testing challenge
head-on and manages to stick it out is mighty
fortunate. For such persons loyally in love
with God, the reward is life and more life.

James 1:12 (MSG)

enjoy words, looking up their origin and exploring their many meanings, discovering new insights
into words and life. That proved true for the word *challenge.* So many of the historical people I write about are
beset with challenges on the Oregon Trail, as homestead-
ers and pioneers, as mothers and fathers making lives for
their families. Challenges are part of the human condition. But when I looked up that word, I found these def-
initions that were familiar: "A call to engage in a fight" or
"the quality of requiring full use of one's abilities, energy, or
resources" or "to summon to action." Quite far down on
Webster's list were origins of the word *challenge* as coming
from the Latin *calumnia,* meaning *trickery.* Right below
that was the definition "to deceive."

How could a challenge be a deception? I began to
think back to a time when I felt challenged. One of the
biggest was finally agreeing to move with my husband to
a remote ranch twenty-five miles from the smallest town,
seven miles from a mailbox and eleven miles from a paved
road. He wanted to build a new life there on 160 acres of
remote sage- and rattlesnake-covered land. After five years
of resistance on my part, we stepped out on a cloud of

faith believing we wouldn't fall through. We faced enormous challenges from the weather, the distance, the isolation. Acquiring building materials, making phone calls from a barn ten miles away, dealing with a treacherous dirt road that wound up a canyon with a 950-foot drop and no guardrails became almost daily encounters with many challenges.

Yet from those challenges my husband and I developed a closer relationship. We found ourselves trusting in God's calling to that land and deepened our loyalty to God. Each of us discovered new skills we didn't realize we had and found ways to help our family that might not so easily have occurred living in suburbia. I found satisfying work on an Indian reservation to supplement our income. I began writing. My husband's son and his wife came to live with us for a time. We found happiness and contentment and more life.

Yet it took me five years to agree to make that move. I was frightened, imagined all the terrible things that could happen (many of them did!), and resisted. I finally relented, and we left our jobs to move to that land only to discover the greatest joys of my life.

The deception in the challenge? If I had stayed where I was, I would never have found that joy; our faith might not have deepened, our lives enriched beyond measure through new professions and helping each other. Sometimes the greatest challenges begin with a deception, our minds telling us, *You can't do that! You're too old, too weak, too foolish.*

Scripture tells us, "Blessed is the one who perseveres under trial." Stepping over the deceit does not mean the challenge will be easy, but doing so promises a deeper relationship with God and the reward of "more life."

God, the Creator of the universe, give us wisdom to see beyond the deceit to the challenge that will deepen our love for You. Help us face the challenges today head-on that we may know You more deeply and discover all You have planned for "more life." Amen.

When our ancestors were in Egypt, they
gave no thought to your miracles; they did
not remember your many kindnesses...
Yet he saved them for his name's sake, to
make his mighty power known.

Psalm 106:7-8

Writer Madeleine L'Engle wrote that "compassion isn't general, it's particular." Compassion in general creates soup kitchens and homeless shelters. Compassion operates orphanages and sustains people on the mission field. Compassion creates hospitals peopled with dedicated physicians and nurses, orderlies and aides.

But compassion is truly known in the particular when the nurse not only removes the bandage and cleans the oozing wound but holds the patient's hand a moment asking, "How are you doing?" It's when a child stops her doll-playing and throws comforting arms around her little friend whose tea set has just broken into a hundred pieces. We recognize compassion as a simple kindness when a neighbor asks if they can run an errand for us while they're out running their own.

The psalmist recalls how fleeting is our recognition of kindness and compassion. I remember reading of the Israelites' flight and of God's providing manna to them daily, leading them by light, rescuing them from bondage. Yet not long after they complained and charged that God had forgotten them, and they returned to their old, familiar gods. "How could they forget all of that?" I remember asking my husband.

But I forget too. That offer of kindness from a neighbor to plow our driveway of a heavy snow. The delivery of a handpicked bouquet from a friend's garden. That card sent for no reason other than to tell us we were remembered. These kindnesses were acknowledged at the time, but days later I feel sorry for myself, wondering where God is in my life. My kindness memory is short-term.

Even worse, I lament God's absence in the larger things, where nations struggle with each other, politics fills the airwaves, unkind words are spoken in coffee shops and on bumper stickers. Where is kindness in this fallen world? Have we forgotten all the kindnesses God has granted? I return to my gods of earning money, disappearing into television, growling about the futility of hoping things could ever change.

But God saves us anyway, the psalmist assures, to make His power known. So when I find myself wondering, as the Hebrews did, where God is, I look for the particular, a way I can act with kindness out of God's love. I'll drive my nephew to work while his car is being fixed even if it is inconvenient. I'll bring that book I promised to my neighbor and spend a little time taking tea with her. For today, I'll look for acts of kindness I can give and acknowledge those given me. Kindness is the humus out of which God's glory can grow.

In the midst of a very severe trial, their
overflowing joy and their extreme
poverty welled up in rich generosity.

2 Corinthians 8:2

I confess I'm rarely happy in a time of trial. Yet Paul writes of the church in the Macedonia province and how their true colors came through in their time of pressure and trouble. Instead of going inward, lamenting their sad state, "they urgently pleaded with us for the privilege of sharing in this service to the Lord's people" (2 Corinthians 8:3). Their joy, even amid deep poverty, overflowed to increase their generosity. How did they do that? How did they draw upon such a spirit that witnessed to their love of Jesus by giving more than they could even afford?

So many of the men and women who pioneered in settling our country decades ago must have discovered that same quality of finding joy in trial, so much joy that it allowed them pass it on, to give generously even when they couldn't afford it. They built barns for neighbors; they raised up schools and churches out of their meager incomes. Today in rural areas neighbors might harvest hay for a farmer who is ill, burning their own fuel and time; and in urban centers a woman grocery shops and keeps a kitchen stocked for a friend weakened by chemotherapy treatments. These generous acts are not done in order to receive joy but because the people have a spirit of God they cannot help but share.

"Generosity," wrote the esteemed psychiatrist Karl Menninger, "is the single most important indicator of a person's mental health. Generous people are rarely mentally ill."

I find those words encouraging not only as a mental health professional but especially as a human being struggling with life's demands and seeing the witness of those who go before me, giving of themselves, in overflowing joy. I pray to be one of them.

*When he rose from prayer and went back
to the disciples, he found them asleep,
exhausted from sorrow…"Get up and pray
so that you do not fall into temptation."*

Luke 22:45-46

xhaustion is a part of grieving. We often fail to
eat. Our sleep—if we have any—is wrought with
twists and turns and a heavy sense of loss when we awake.
Tears, while helping us to heal, also deplete our bodies.
The natural elixirs of healing and hope sink deep into our
beings, and we often lack the energy to bring them forth.
Perhaps this is why when Jesus found His friends in the
sleep of sorrow, He awoke them with direction, that they
might pray and with God's strength defeat the temptation to give in to grief, to let it consume them into despair.
Jesus knew what lay ahead for Him and for them, and He
knew they'd need God's strength to withstand the time of
sorrow and demand that they would face.

I like to think Jesus said those words with kindness to
His friends, understanding how sorrow takes us to places
we would never imagine we might go. Yet comforting others in a time of loss can be almost more troubling than
grieving our own losses and disappointments.

"Grief is the price we have to pay for loving," some wise
sage said. Helping another grieve can be like walking on
lily pads where, with one misstep, one could sink at any
moment to the bottom. But God is there reminding us
to get up, take that step, and pray through the exhaustion.

"She has done a beautiful thing to me."

Mark 14:6

A woman poured expensive oil over the feet of Jesus. This generous act received much criticism from the witnesses in Simon the Leper's house. "This expensive perfume could have been sold and helped many in need," some of those present said. But Jesus corrected them and said, "She has done a beautiful thing to me."

F. Dean Lueking, in *Christian Century* magazine, notes that the Greek Mark used in this passage, variously translated as "good service" or "beautiful thing," is not *agathos*, "implying utility and moral correctness, but *kalos*, implying something not only good but lovely, gracefully winsome in its uniqueness." That Jesus should note the importance of *kalos* in this woman's act pleases me.

Sometimes creative acts such as arranging flowers, quilting a wall hanging, painting a picture, writing a poem, baking bread to share are diminished in society's eyes—and sometimes even in the eyes of their producer. The giving of cut flowers when someone feels discouraged is a "beautiful thing." When a child grants us a picture for our refrigerator, that's a "beautiful thing," no less valued than someone's gift of a bag of groceries to fill a sparse cupboard.

In some ways the Proverbs 31 woman is a contradiction to this woman of Mark's verse. The Proverbs 31 woman does everything for her family, is never idle, makes money, and brings praise from her husband and her children. Would she ever pour expensive perfume over the feet of Jesus? I can't picture her doing so. But I love the image of a woman who did, one who like many of us doesn't feel up to the standards of that amazing woman of Proverbs but who wants to do something lovely, gracefully winsome in a unique act of generosity, and in so doing might bring on the blessing of Jesus saying, "She has done a beautiful thing to me."

I hope this day I will give extravagantly as Jesus gives to each of us. My prayer is to give in such a way that others are blessed not only with the practicality of my gift but with the pureness of heart that says, "This may be fleeting, but it is meant to bring beauty and loveliness into your world." Let me be aware of those gifts of beauty given each day to me. May I daily thank God for doing something beautiful that restores me and allows me to give to others in a lovely *kalos* way.

Love is patient, love is kind.

1 Corinthians 13:4

I'd told him three times, answering the same question. He even says, "I know you've told me, but where is it we're going again?" I find myself impatient, snapping the answer. "To your neurologist appointment. See, I wrote it on the board."

Yes, we've tried any number of tips to help address the problem of memory loss and confusion that can come with a stroke, even a mild one. Or it may even be a result of our just growing older. Truth is, I sometimes forget and have to ask *him* the same question more than once.

If love is patient and kind, then why am I not patient? Why am I not kinder? I truly do love my husband. Sometimes I worry that the love has disappeared into a caring kind of emotion, where the deep-felt love has been weakened by the challenges we've faced. I leave those conversations carrying guilt as heavy as the laundry basket that never seems to empty.

But then I read the Scripture again. Love is patient and kind, and that means God's love toward me is patient and kind too. God understands my human limits and offers, if I ask for a renewed look at love, a reminder of its sacrifice. The guilt can spur me on to make some small, personal change. I am human, and there will be days when I am frustrated and impatient. God assures me that

He will never say, "I've told you a thousand times, I will never leave you nor forsake you."

I can take a deep breath and begin again. "It's your appointment," I tell my husband, knowing he can't help but ask the question. I'll just leave out how many times I may have told him, already reflecting God's patience and kindness toward me.

Praise be to the God and Father of our Lord
Jesus Christ, the Father of compassion
and the God of all comfort, who comforts
us in all our troubles, so that we can
comfort those in any trouble with the
comfort we ourselves receive from God.

2 Corinthians 1:3-4

For seventeen years I worked on the Warm Springs Indian reservation in Central Oregon, assisting families who had children with special needs. I remember one young girl whose father brought her weekly to a small group to work on her speech concerns. She was exceedingly shy. When her birthday arrived, the small group of children and their parents planned a celebration. Her father brought a cake with candles, and other sweet goodies added to the festive plates and napkins and balloons that lined the child's table in the classroom at the Early Childhood Center. All went well until the group began to sing "Happy Birthday" to Julia. Instead of beaming in the attention, her eyes grew large and tearful, and she slowly slid from her chair to hide under the table.

I felt so sad for her and didn't know exactly what to do. But I needn't have worried. The children knew. One by one, they too slid under the table to sit with her and just be.

I've never forgotten this act of compassion, spontaneously enacted by these children who demonstrated what I think God seeks for each of us when we encounter someone in need. Just be where they are and walk beside them. Compassion is composed of the prefix *com,* which in Latin means "with," and *pati,* "to bear, suffer." That's what the children did, and their sympathetic act eventually brought Julia out from under the table to finish her party, the honoree fully assured that she was not alone.

How gracious is our God who is with us, especially as we walk beside those needing care, guidance, support, and encouragement. May I remember that this day and be willing to slide beneath a table to bring comfort.

And Jesus grew in wisdom and stature,
and in favor with God and man.

Luke 2:52

Some years ago I was asked to lead a women's retreat having to do with stress reduction. I was a mental health counselor, and it seemed reasonable that I might know something about the issues of stress. As I prepared, this verse became my outline, a model for the facets of our lives where we can make changes to bring renewed energy and vigor to our days despite the challenges.

Our minds have much to do with our stress. How we see a challenge greatly affects how stressful the event may be.

When my father was dying from congestive heart failure and dealing with dementia, one evening in the middle of the night he called out my name. I came to him, and as I leaned over his hospital bed, he grabbed my hand and said, "How will I know when to go?" My heart ached with the knowledge that he knew, too, that his time of ending this life was near. Somehow words formed. "They'll come for you," I told him. "You'll recognize Jesus, and then there'll be Judy [his daughter] and your parents and your brothers and your sister Palma. They're all there waiting for you, and you'll simply lean back into the arms of Jesus, and you'll know it is time to go." He smiled and patted my hand.

A day later, he went into a coma, but I was there to

hear his final recognizable words. His face lit up, and he smiled and said, "Palma!" As much as I hated the thought of losing him, I was so encouraged by his question. Even in the midst of his dying, he brought wisdom to me for my passage when that time comes.

*And Jesus grew in **wisdom** and stature,*
and in favor with God and man.

Luke 2:52

How we are is how we see. Some of us see the glass half full; others see the glass half empty. The reality I'm struck by is that the same event or object can be seen in many different ways. We can reduce our stress by thinking differently about the events, actually changing how we feel.

The death of my father was agonizing, but I could find the blessing within it by the gift God gave of my father's last word being the name of his sister. When my husband had his stroke and heart attack within ten days of each other, I could thank God that we were only twelve minutes from a cardiac center instead of on our remote ranch twenty-five miles from the nearest community clinic. My mind allowed me to seek out wisdom within the stressful events, looking for the gift, changing how I felt from fear and anxiety to gratitude. We had moved just five months earlier, a decision made quickly, though at the time we didn't know why. Once Jerry had his health problems, we understood.

We enrich our lives as we grow in wisdom through Scripture reading, through prayer, through group discussions about belief and behavior as Christians. Trusting that I can actually change how I feel (even when I'd like to think if I dislike something, I *always* will) is an act of wisdom. Where once I was impatient, I can talk to myself in ways that remind me that Jesus grew in wisdom by becoming closer to God. It did not reduce the demands on His life and ministry, but seeing the world through God's eyes allowed Him to model wisdom for His disciples that they too might continue to grow.

*And Jesus grew in wisdom and **stature**,*
and in favor with God and man.

Luke 2:52

What is stature? I think it's our physical being, the temple of our body and how we treat it. Jesus grew in stature, in His bodily strength necessary to complete His ministry on this earth. I suspect He did not overindulge in dates filled with sweet honey nor did He spend days as a couch potato simply gazing out over the Sea of Galilee. We know He didn't have time for crossword puzzles, though doing them does quicken the mind, I've heard. Jesus was active, walking long distances, His strong voice carrying His message of hope out onto the boats and along the shoreline filled with hurting souls seeking new life. He is a model for good health and increasing in stature.

In my own life, stress is greatly reduced when I have an active physical routine. Sometimes it means taking the dogs for a walk. It may be an exercise program for both my husband and me. Jerry's routine helps his heart recovery; mine keeps my mind and body alert and able to tend to his needs as well as my own. How well we plan our meals and the kinds of foods we eat all contribute to our stature. Choosing a hike over a television program may take effort, but the results help reduce stress and allow each of us to be stronger in our spiritual walk.

If your life is filled with stressful days, giving yourself permission to grow in stature, to pay attention to your body's needs and not just that of your loved one, is an act of spiritual growth sanctioned by Jesus' life.

And Jesus grew in wisdom and stature,
*and in favor with **God** and man.*

Luke 2:52

Oh to grow in favor with God! How dear that must have been for Jesus as He grew into His ministry on this earth. To be called forward and at His baptism to hear the words, "You are my Son, whom I love; with you I am well pleased" (Mark 1:11), is a commendation each of us might long for.

Yet we fall short as humans. We always do. Still, the prodigal son returned to the open arms of his father fully forgiven for his wayward ways. And the brother, the one who had his father's love all along, he stood back and found he had to deal with the stress of his envy, with figuring out how to grow in a new way in his father's favor. He struggled to find a way to receive the gift of his father who loved him just as much as he loved the prodigal. Sometimes being a recipient is more stressful than being the giver.

Sometimes I fear that my work to "achieve" is overshadowed by my ability to "receive." In caring for others, I can easily give, sometimes with resentment but more often with joy, seeing the privilege for what it is. But there is much more for me to do in receiving. If I have trouble accepting the gratitude of a friend I've helped or in acknowledging without discounting a compliment from another meant to encourage, however will

I grow in favor with God? However will I receive His blessings when He whispers in my ear, "With you I am well pleased"?

I must practice opening my arms and allowing God to pull me to Him.

And Jesus grew in wisdom and stature,
*and in favor with God and **man**.*

Luke 2:52

esus grew in favor with those around Him. Most stressful situations are tangled up in relationships. Arguments over property between fathers and sons. Disagreements over who received the necklace raging for years between daughters after a mother's passing. Feuds in churches over worship practices, the pastor's child who runs around the church undisciplined, the "terrible color of the carpet" chosen by the committee. How many times have we resigned from a committee over a hurt feeling, allowing a damaged relationship to interfere with the work God has called us to do?

I try to imagine Jesus dealing with relationship issues. We know He did. John and James asking for special favors; Peter denying Him when confronted by a servant girl; the likely comments of His disciples after He spoke to the woman at the well, whose reputation was not the sort to warrant the Son of God's attention.

And yet we know He grew in favor with men, and I would dare say with women as well. He turned a listening ear to the hurting. He paid attention to the pain behind the touch of the bleeding woman. He asked the blind man what he really wanted, not assuming He knew. He received the blessings of the woman with the expensive perfume. He told us the poor would always be with us, but He did not say that entitled us to ignore them, reminding us that as we did to the least of these, we did to Him. He reminded us of the Old Testament model of what the Lord requires: to love mercy, seek justice, and walk humbly with our God.

Years ago the research on how we respond to stress gave us two words: *fight* or *flight*. The research was done with mostly college sophomore men. Now the research is being done with female subjects, and the words *tend* and *befriend* materialize. That seems fitting for how to grow in our relationships even during times of challenge: tend and befriend, as Jesus did.

Books, prayers, discussions with counselors, daily devotions, support groups, songs of praise and adoration, journaling, and soaking in Scripture all guide my relationships. Jesus is still the model to keep growing, learning new ways to communicate, to say I'm sorry, to express love, and seek wisdom to step over the day-to-day annoyances that unchecked can lead to bigger problems or to give them up and find the gift within.

*Whether you turn to the right or to the
left, your ears will hear a voice behind
you, saying, "This is the way; walk in it."*

Isaiah 30:21

he local paper reported a change for people who
like to drive or hike in National Forest Service
areas. In the future, all the old signs of road closures or
openings would be taken down. Instead, people would be
given as many as thirteen maps to keep them from driving on a closed road (and risking a fine) or safely maneu-
vering the roads that are open.

I like maps, even old ones found in musty geography
and history books. Maps are made to help us find our
way but also to reduce the fear of the unknown. Looking after someone else, caring for their health, making
decisions sometimes alone because they're not able to
help decide, makes me want a good map. I want a way
to "find my way" and not get lost. I also long to set the
fear of the unknown aside. I don't want to get lost on
this journey.

Scripture offers a map, not perhaps in specific ways
that might keep us from driving on a closed road and
risking a fine. But the stories, the promises, the hope,
and history of Scripture show us the way. In the process,
the understanding of what others chose and how they

managed in the wilderness reminds us that we need not fear. The map of God's love is clear.

Today, that will be my map when I face a closed road or wonder what lies ahead. I'll trust that I am not alone on my journey. The map of Scripture awaits.

You brought us to a place of abundance.

Psalm 66:12

A poem by Robert Frost, "Two Look at Two," is about a couple taking a hike up a hillside. They reach the top and see the splendor of the view, and the poet says, "'This is all,' they sighed. But there was more." Out of the trees came a deer on porcelain legs, ears pointed in their direction but not moving away in fear. They shared the space. The poet writes: "'This, then, is all. What more is there to ask?' But, no, not yet." Another thing emerges from the woods: a buck with its regal stand.

There are days of delight in my life when I spy the first daffodil of spring and I think to myself, *This is all.* But then there is more. A chipmunk slips inside the rock wall; the dog nudges my leg begging for a walk; my husband reminds me of a time on the ranch when he awoke me at 2:00 a.m. to step out onto a February porch and view a magenta sky split with streaks of black dotted with stars. The aurora borealis had come to our doorstep. We'd gone to bed saying to ourselves it was the end of the day.

"'This is all,' they sighed; But there was more."

The phrase will be the reminder to savor the small joys of the day—and to wait for more. It is my prayer that when those I love leave this life that I will remember the poet: "'This is all,' they sighed. But there was more."

In God, there is always more.

God had planned something better for us.

Hebrews 11:40

lone in the cool emergency room, I wait for the results of the X-rays, the day's schedule now totally erased. I pray that nothing is broken from the fall my husband took down ten cement steps in a hotel far from home. But I chafe at the many changes we will need to make in the upcoming plans.

It's on days like this that I strain to trust the Scripture that "God had planned something better for us." Instead I feel guilty that I didn't hang on to Jerry's hand to keep him from falling. I'm annoyed that he didn't hold the railing. I regret that I didn't say something about how wobbly he seemed in the morning, his balance still not quite right since his stroke. I feel sorry for myself that now I'll have to do all the driving and lifting; then beg for forgiveness for my selfish ways while he lies on the X-ray table. When we return home we'll need to confer with his doctors about the change in medicine that might have made him unstable. Whatever we had planned will have to wait. This caregiving is not for the fainthearted.

He returns and nothing is broken! His arm is badly sprained and bruised and he's lost flesh. I'll need to learn how to change the bandage. His hip is sore; his jaw already starting to turn black and blue. But he can walk! He never lost consciousness. I'll let friends know, and they will pray for rapid healing.

Hours later, we walk out into a rainy day. He gets inside the car. I pull the seat belt over his chest and hook it, and we drive toward adjusted plans, trusting that God has planned something better for us.

"I was a stranger and you invited me in."

Matthew 25:35

esterday Jerry became so ill we left the sanctuary in the middle of the sermon. His head pounded and while he has a high pain tolerance, this headache was worse than he'd experienced since he'd broken his neck thirty years before. We had to bother the people sitting at the end of the pew; they offered to come and help, but we declined, hoping to make as little disruption as possible in this large congregation we've been a part of for less than two years. In the foyer, Jerry sat with his head down. Someone went for a glass of water, and then he was ready for me to take him home where cold packs rotated with a heating pad for several hours until the headache ceased.

But here's the thing that touched me—a phone message we received at home from the people we'd disturbed as we left the sanctuary. We'd just met them, only knew their first names. They'd had to find out who we were and then make a call just to follow up, wanting to be certain Jerry was all right. Listening to the message brought tears to my eyes.

The words of Epicurus, an ancient philosopher of the third century BC, came to mind: "It is not so much our friends' help that helps us as the confident knowledge that they will help us." Help came from strangers, and I felt as though I was the outsider and these people had invited us in. It is a reminder to be open to the unknown…and to return the gift and invite strangers in to extend the relationship that is the family of God.

My own vineyard I have not kept!

Song of Songs 1:6 (NRSV)

When we lived on the ranch, we planted a vineyard. It required daily tending, constant checking, and during certain seasons, we asked for help to keep up with the labor-intensive task of growing grapes. We had to change our routines when it was time to prune or harvest. Vineyards require that; so do marriages.

The days of stress have taken their toll, and the price has been loss of intimacy. Too fatigued to consider the joys of touching or being close. Too angry, too guilty, too frightened about the future. Too disinterested. Our own vineyard neglected.

Intimacy does not need to be a casualty of illness, trials, or loss, but it does require the same intensity as a vineyard to keep it flourishing. It requires first the admission that something nourishing has left the relationship and that God as lover wishes it were not so. He draws us to Him that we might not ignore the vineyard. That is reason enough for us to trust that He will help us restore the field to flourishing blooms, giving us the energy and interest to do so.

My beloved is to me a cluster of henna
blossoms from the vineyards of En Gedi.

Song of Songs 1:1-4

n Gedi is an oasis watered by a spring near the
Dead Sea. I love this image that something beautiful and nourishing is found in the midst of a desert, close
to a sea that allows little more than floating in its salt-
laden water. The Dead Sea has no outlet. It takes in water
from the streams flowing from the mountains of Herman,
but the water has nowhere to go once it enters the Dead
Sea. Yet not far away is an oasis that Scripture says brought
about henna blossoms that are aromatic, giving pleasure
to all who find respite at this site.

When relationships falter, when intimacy and closeness with or without sexual contact disappear because our
energies are given over to the demands of caring, to the
details of doctor appointments or the necessities of grocery shopping and paying bills, we may forget to seek that
oasis. Instead, I sometimes feel like I'm floating in the
Dead Sea, going nowhere, and without even the pleasure
of remembering a time when caring meant a gentle touch,
a smile and flirting eyes that brought about true intimacy.

So today, I'll have that conversation, expressing my
fatigue but also a desire to rediscover closeness. Today, I'll
ask that he turn off the television, look into my eyes, hold
my hands, and for just a moment we might caress each

other's cheeks and appreciate the wrinkles leading to our eyes that may lack the sparkle of times before but still hold the promise of a life everlasting.

It may be for only a moment, but those simple acts serve as henna blossoms from a nourishing place.

"I am unworthy of all the kindness and
faithfulness you have shown your servant."

Genesis 32:10

The word *unworthy* can mean "to think little of"
or to consider oneself "small and insignificant."
Neither are qualities that would enable the disciples to do
the work Jesus called them to. In that wilderness place of
uncertainty and fear as they waited in Jerusalem for the
promised coming of the Spirit, those disciples must have
felt unworthy. Just as Moses did when he was called to
lead his people out of bondage.

Yet surely to feel insignificant or to think little of oneself is a barrier to all the good works God wants us to
do and for all the good things God wants for us. Being
unworthy drains us of vitality and hope. There are days I
feel unworthy, don't believe I'm capable of giving the kind
of care that stabilizes another's life let alone enriches it.

I'm reminded of a friend who took her mother into
her home to live with her in her last months of life. She
reached for my friend's hand and said, "I don't know
how I'll be." Such a poignant understanding even in her
dementia! None of us knows how we'll be when the time
comes for us to need close tending by another. I have no
idea if I'll be the salt water queen of the Dead Sea or if
the caring side of me will flow out like water to the Sea of
Galilee. I have my doubts about the latter. I think myself
unworthy of the gift of compassion.

Therein lies the trial. If we're to do the Lord's work, we must see ourselves as worthy. Sometimes I'm reminded to look toward the goal: what was it I was called to do? I was called to care for another "in sickness and in health." I was called to honor my father and mother—in sickness and in health too, I suspect. I am called to do what the Lord commands: "to act justly and to love mercy and to walk humbly with your God." I can't do any of that without first finding the worth within me, the worth God gave. To remain insignificant is to reject the gift and turn my back on the task.

Thank God the disciples found a way to give up their sense of unworthiness that must have hovered over them like a black cloud of insects in that room while they waited, being obedient. Otherwise the great ministry Jesus had started might have died for lack of worthy workers. I'll remember that. It's not about my worthiness…it's about the task assigned. And I am not alone on the journey.

There are different kinds of gifts, but the
same Spirit distributes them. There are
different kinds of service, but the same Lord.

1 Corinthians 12:4-5

It really wouldn't have worked to have my parents—with their many health needs—come to live with us on our remote ranch. An assisted-living facility on the reservation where I worked seemed wisest. A year or so later my father died. My older sister had died several years before, and my brother lived two thousand miles away. That left my mom and me.

Guilt for not bringing her to live with me was a constant. Rationally, I knew being hours from her doctor made no sense. I also knew she had friends at her assisted-living facility. She continued to be in service, reading to others whose sight failed. She even volunteered at the reservation Head Start program. She had a giving life, and moving her to be with me would have taken that from her and kept her from the emergency medical care she often needed.

But the truth was that my mom and I were like two magnets trying to connect but always having a force that kept us apart. After my father died and my mom lived alone in the assisted-living apartment, I knew I wanted to break that force. But moving her to be with me was not the answer. How to "put [my] religion into practice by caring" (1 Timothy 5:4), that was the struggle—until I read Paul's words one morning: "There are different kinds of gifts, but the same Spirit distributes them. There are different kinds of service, but the same Lord."

I would do what I could do best: to be with her, listen to her, laugh with her while ensuring she had a safe and loving place to live. It was all right to allow others to serve her with their gifts and for me to find a way to bring joy to her life through my gifts. That would be my way of putting my religion into practice, and I prayed it would be "pleasing to God."

"If I only touch his cloak, I will be healed."

Matthew 9:21

T hose last months before my mother died were filled with what I call scratchy gifts. I wasn't her direct caregiver, but I was there, caring. Early on, her grief at my father's death came out as irritation. She was annoyed at me, at the food served, at the staff. As a retired nurse, she complained they weren't checking her blood-sugar level and didn't believe me until I showed her the used strips in her wastepaper basket.

One day she was so frustrated with me that I sat her down and said, "Look. Dad is gone. Your daughter Judy is gone. Your only son lives far away. So you are stuck with me, and we have to find a way to make this work now that it's just the two of us."

She lowered her head. "I don't think I'm stuck with you," she said.

I know the words must have been hard to hear. She was of a generation that didn't feel the need for self-reflection, and she'd raised a daughter who became a therapist! That interchange affected us though. After that, she began reaching out for me when I'd come into her apartment. She was not a hugger or toucher, so that was new. We'd watch her favorite television shows together, and I stopped looking at my watch suggesting I didn't have time. I made time. I'd pay her bills, and we'd laugh about a conversation she'd had about wearing hats. I like hats and I didn't realize that she did too. I began to see her with new eyes.

While looking through an old photograph album one evening, I noticed something unique in all the photographs of my mother and me: we were never touching. I'm not sure why that was. She'd had many illnesses and surgeries as a child, so perhaps touching meant pain. I decided then that while she never touched me in a photograph, I didn't want her to leave this world without my having a picture of me touching her.

The day came. We were at an outdoor concert together in a little town halfway between her care facility and our ranch. She'd spent the weekend with us, and we were taking her back after the concert. It was very hot with little shade. I had two hats in the car: one a black cowboy hat and the other a straw hat. She donned the cowboy hat, I donned the other, and someone took our picture. Her hands were folded in her lap. I had my arm around her, touching her. Six months later, she died, but that picture of touching her brings healing to me every time I see it.

I thank God each day I made the time to know her, shifted the magnet so we were drawn together even if it took long years. And I thank God for the healing that came from my touching her.

*"Blessed are those who mourn, for
they will be comforted."*

Matthew 5:4

Mourning doesn't happen only with a death. It happens with a change—sometimes happy ones—and loss. A child moves out; an adult child moves in. A baby arrives, a joyous event but still requiring major adjustments. We mourn what once was. Grief has many siblings. Anger, guilt, unworthiness, and sadness all show up for the reunion.

My father's dementia moved him in and out of reason and the present. For my mom, knowing what had once been and seeing how he now was made her angry and upset. "He's being silly," she'd complain when he told me that aliens fueled their spaceships from the rock outside their apartment's window. "He knows better." Once I asked her what she'd do with a patient who acted like Dad (she was a retired nurse), and she said, "Just agree with them. They don't know any better. It's the disease." She sighed. "It's just that he was so much more and now he's this."

As we come to terms with what is, we walk the path of mourning. Sometimes there are treatments or alternatives to assist us as we face the challenges, but ultimately it is our capacity to mourn and then accept the blessings that will bring us comfort.

As I walk this path of change, I will remember the verse of Matthew and take time to mourn, for only then will I find comfort.

*Lord, you alone are my portion and my
cup; you make my lot secure. The boundary
lines have fallen for me in pleasant places;
surely I have a delightful inheritance.*

Psalm 16:5-6

I define *wilderness* as those places where we find ourselves where we'd really rather not be. Caring for an aging parent, an ill husband, a struggling child is often just such a wilderness place. A job lost, a family member moving in, even a promotion can be a wilderness for a time.

We didn't plan for Jerry's illnesses or falls or surgeries; they happened, taking us both out of routine and into uncertainty. When I admit I'm there, I find comfort in knowing that God has promised to maintain my lot and that these new boundaries He sees as pleasant places.

When I can look through God's eyes at our current state, the corrals, the arena of my life becomes wider and fear of the unknown lessens. Instead of seeing anxiety and guilt and fear before me, I can rest at least for a moment or two, allowing God to show me His vision.

Now if only I will let Him.

> *"Ask and it will be given to you;*
> *seek and you will find; knock and*
> *the door will be opened to you."*
>
> *Luke 11:9*

Caring for loved ones in their final stages of transition from this life to more life can be both challenging and filled with grace. My father had a kind of dementia that allowed him sometimes to be perfectly coherent, aware of events and memories as clear as a younger man. Then he'd disappear from us into a world of his own. The transition could happen within the same sentence. We learned to "go with the flow" of his mind that, like a stream of water, sometimes disappeared underground, reappearing miles downstream.

My mother's last days following a stroke were a transition. After a visit with the speech and occupational therapist, she asked, "How bad is it?"

"Your left side is all involved," I told her. "But everyone is hopeful that with effort and time, you'll be back." She nodded. "Like Fern," she said, referring to her older sister who had spent long months in a nursing home following a major stroke.

The next day she had a heart attack, but she could still speak. I'd called my brother to fly west to be with us. "How bad is it?" she asked, and I told her. "You can come back. You have before." She nodded. And then, words came I had not planned to say. "But you don't have to." I held her hand. "We don't want you to leave us, but you may be tired and ready to go on to new life. That's your choice, and we'll love you through it and miss you when you're gone." She nodded. "Tell your brother to hurry."

My brother did arrive in time to hold her, tell her he loved her, and for us to be there when she turned her head to the pillow where her tape recorder played "Softly and Tenderly Jesus Is Calling" and passed on to more life.

"How bad is it?" she'd asked. And with the answer, she had chosen not to fight to stay in this world. Those who loved her could give by allowing her to leave and holding each other—not her—in our grief.

A cheerful heart is good medicine.

Proverbs 17:22

Today I'm sick. A cough has dragged on for weeks and taken its toll on my energy, cheerfulness, and goodwill. I'm irritable and snapping at my husband, feeling put upon by his sprained arm adding to the cardiac recovery, crushed vertebrae, and other things his body has to daily tackle. I take the garbage out. Bandage his arm from the wounds suffered when he fell. His neck and hip are still black and blue, so I know he is in worse shape than I am. But fatigue and resentment surround my duties.

By day's end I am remorseful, asking for prayers that I might be a better person.

In my caregiver support group the next day, a woman describes my emotional state and says she prays to be a better person. Her friend beside her says she never prays to be better: "I pray for God to make my husband better." We all laughed and that felt good. We'd all been in that place feeling put upon, wishing what was so, wasn't.

But what is, is. That's the challenge: to accept what is while still hoping for a bit of change in the direction we desire. For there will always be change, and we can better accept it on cheerful days. Laughter is good medicine, not just for those we care for but for the caregivers as well.

They were all together in one place.

Acts 2:1

The disciples dutifully waited in Jerusalem as our Lord had told them. They were frightened. Some were in legal trouble. Those days before the Holy Spirit descended upon them must have been filled with anxiety and fear. Jesus was no longer among them; they lived in an unknown wilderness place.

What might have helped them endure this uncertain time? Togetherness, for one thing. They were all together in one place. Friends, supportive family, people from our neighborhood or church whom we allow to help us can ease the burden of the unknown.

Often we decline to let others assist us. How many times have we said, "No, I can do it," to an offer to pick up groceries for us or spend an hour freeing us to take a walk or run an errand without having to actually "run."

We give a gift when we are all together in one place and when we allow others to give to us. I like to believe Jesus' disciples understood that receiving the support of others was a gift to the giver. It's my reminder the next time someone says, "Let me do that for you." I'll let them.

*But Samuel replied: "Does the LORD
delight in burnt offerings and sacrifices
as much as in obeying the LORD? To
obey is better than sacrifice..."*

1 Samuel 15:22

When in wilderness places, I pray to do what the disciples did before the day of Pentecost: they obeyed. They did what Jesus told them to do and waited. It is one of the behaviors that helps us move through challenging places: being obedient in a time of trial.

For me that often looks like sticking to daily routines. Having time in Scripture even when I feel rushed—perhaps especially when I'm feeling rushed. Sarah Wesley, the mother of John and Charles, had seventeen children to care for. On days she knew there'd be much to do, it's said she spent even more time with her morning Scriptures and prayer. That's what obedience looks like.

Making myself take walks to listen for God's voice—if only for ten minutes—is being obedient. Giving to another in need, that is being obedient. As a caregiver, we need brief moments every day that can restore us so we don't become depleted. Sitting on the garden swing while I have tasks to accomplish can be as obedient as prayer. Both renew the spirit.

When I feel myself frightened, worried about what will happen next, losing control, I am reminded of Samuel's words of what delights the Lord: not sacrifices as much as listening to God's voice and obeying it. God wants us nurtured by the Holy Spirit, and as with the disciples before Pentecost, they first had to surrender and be obedient and wait for that day of joy to descend upon them.

But now you have had every stain washed
off: now you have been set apart as holy:
now you have been pronounced free from
guilt; in the name of our Lord Jesus Christ
and through the Spirit of our God.

1 Corinthians 6:11 (WEY)

*M*uch guilt rests on my shoulders, growing heavier by the day. I'm not as good a caregiver as I'd like to be. I'm annoyed by little things instead of stepping over them. Regrets for not understanding my mom, sister, father, granddaughter better now settle on me like a cold, suffocating snow. I wonder how Peter lived with his guilt. We know how Judas chose to deal with his.

When the disciples gathered in Jerusalem after Jesus's resurrection, they must have found a way to deal with their past deplorable actions—of denying Jesus, of arguing over petty things like who would sit where in heaven while so many more important challenges faced them. Perhaps little guilts worked on them like sand in a sandal, irritating, causing pain to distract from grief and loss and change. Each disciple had to put the past behind him if he was going to move forward carrying out Jesus' mission.

I look to those disciples and their friends on days when guilt reigns. Regret that can move us toward a change in action is a healthy thing. But guilt detains us, keeps us carrying rocks from here to there with no hope of ever giving up our load. Memories are not meant to hold us hostage but to transform us.

Today's Scripture reminds us that if we ask, we are forgiven. Every stain is washed off. We are pronounced free from guilt if we will but allow it. Paul says to forget and reach forward.

I take a deep sigh, pray for that washing, and remind myself that I am doing the best I can and that my husband is doing the best he can too. Neither of us ever starts our day saying, "I think I'll be grumpy and irritable and carry around rocks of guilt." We start, hoping to do the best we can. We can do more only with God's help.

When he was at the table with them,
he took bread, gave thanks, broke
it and began to give it to them.

Luke 24:30

A few days after the attacks on the World Trade Center, I had a book signing scheduled. People weren't gathering in public places much, but we decided to go ahead. It was in Portland, Oregon, and more than 125 appeared, perhaps seeking comfort from shared grief.

The last woman to have her book signed told me a story to remember. A Pakistani couple lived at the end of her street, and she noticed that since the attacks they had never left their home. "How frightened they must be," she told me. "I wondered what I could do. I asked myself, *What would Jane's characters do?*" She couldn't understand their language; they'd never met. But she decided she could bake bread, which is what she did, taking it down the street and ringing their doorbell. They served her tea, and with limited language skills, they broke bread together and formed a bridge to friendship in a time of peril.

In their own wilderness places, the disciples also broke bread with each other and the others, men and women, who waited with them. In Spanish, *com pan* means "with bread," but the Spanish is also a bridge to the word *companion* and even *compassion.* At one time the preface *com* meant "to exchange burdens," and surely that's what breaking bread together can do.

Jerry and I now eat with the television off. It's hard to break bread and have a spiritual renewal with 24/7 news feeds blaring in the background. We attempt to cook together. We watch each other so we don't burn the chicken again (such a terrible loss!) or leave the rice pudding on the bottom of the pan, now black as the dog's nose. We excuse ourselves from speaking of trials or worries when serving gluten-free sandwiches and venison stew.

We're getting better about attending church dinners, too, where we'll meet new people even though neither of us does well with those early connections. The bread breaks and so do the knots in our hearts. For just a time, we are breaking bread together, bringing newness into our lives, a richness that breaks routine and reminds us of the disciples doing likewise during their wilderness time.

"These people are not drunk, as you suppose. It's only nine in the morning!"

Acts 2:15

On that day of Pentecost, the Holy Spirit descended on the disciples, and they spoke in tongues and must have danced around in joyous ecstasy, the Breath of the Holy Spirit swirling them like wind in a pile of yellow maple leaves. The followers of Jesus "let go" so much so that Peter felt the need to explain to others what was going on!

When my mother lay dying, friends visited every hour. The dog arrived to lick her face. We had music playing— her favorite hymns. While the rest of us stood around her bed listening to the change in her breathing, we shared stories of my mother's funny sayings, the times when we had all laughed together despite the circumstances. One summer she broke both her wrists by falling on two separate days. Not funny! But feeding her and listening to her make jokes about her sudden disability could make us all smile and appreciate this octogenarian.

At the luncheon following my grandmother's funeral, we all laughed in the church basement and told stories. We didn't see it as sacrilegious; we were letting go, transferring culture by sharing the stories with the next generation.

Peter's need for explanation suggests a rousing, unusual time for the disciples. They were being visited by the Holy Spirit who blows us around without pattern.

I believe they were also experiencing the great joy that comes with relief, with a direction and the courage to take the next step on their faith journey. The word *celebrate* means "to fill up with joy," and it suggests that it be done over and over. As caregivers, we often don't make time for rousing good times, to celebrate by filling up with gratitude, with the gifts of time that others may give us, with laughter during a caregiver support group. That's one reason why I attend! One way to move through a wilderness place is by seeking joy in everyday things.

Surely the disciples that day had an amazing, theologically profound experience with the Holy Spirit. Their acceptance of that anointing renewed their courage for the task ahead. That they had smiles on their faces and joy in their hearts is evidence that we need such celebrations too.

Many are the plans in a person's heart, but it is the LORD's purpose that prevails.

Proverbs 19:21

It's now two weeks out from Jerry's fall down concrete steps at a hotel we were staying at in the middle of a book tour. He missed the first step and down he went. He had the presence of mind to curl himself. (I would have likely fallen splat on my face!) I was sure his arm and possibly his hip were broken and worried that his back might have been reinjured as well. While he was whisked off to the X-ray, I sat in the emergency room and tried to figure out whether to have the surgery there or take him back to Bend. I tried to imagine how to rearrange the book tour, giving me time to get him safely to surgery and to tend him afterward.

Amazingly, though he's eighty-two, he had no broken bones! A sprained left arm, lots of lost skin, a bruised shoulder and hip, and a sprained neck as well. I'm sure the fall did little for his already bad back, but he's gotten through it.

We've gotten through it.

And I learned something about planning. I sat in that ER trying to decide where Jerry should have his surgery. That was wasted time. He didn't need surgery. Prayers, deep breathing, a bit of calm in the storm would have been more productive.

Sometimes in my effort to get all my ducks in a row, I instead add new ducks that don't need to be there. Later, they quack away, mocking me for my "plans."

Proverbs reminds us of that. I appear to need constant reminders.

Turn to me and be gracious to me,
for I am lonely and afflicted.

Psalm 25:16

After Jerry's stroke his eyes were vacant, as though the mind of the man I'd married thirty-five years before no longer lived with me. He spoke little as speech was difficult, and mostly his words were to help meet his needs: getting him the spoon he wanted; telling me he was cold. The dogs bumped their noses against his knees, and sometimes he reached down to pet them, but mostly he sat, stared at something I couldn't see.

After he stabilized and the critical health concerns were met, I had time to ponder what had happened and how much more there was yet to happen. Would I now have to manage everything alone? I tried not to panic anticipating what might never come to pass. But one day, while eating at the table with my silent friend beside me, I felt the weight of loneliness, the despair of the psalmist crying "Turn to me, be gracious to me, for I am lonely and afflicted."

Being lonely felt heavy as a stone I wasn't certain I could lift by myself. What had happened in a heartbeat to a relationship, a friend, someone I loved? I called a friend, and as helpful as it was to speak with her and take in her encouraging words, the loneliness persisted through grocery shopping, fixing meals, even taking the dogs for a walk.

The childhood hymn that came to me in an hour of

deep despair was "What a Friend We Have in Jesus." The poetry of the words returned me to a time when I felt God "turn to me" like an intimate friend who filled my lonely childhood with hopefulness and peace. That will be my prayer today, to revisit times before when I felt God turn to me and trust that God never turned away. God is with me and my husband, the stranger who sits quietly beside me.

Look at me and help me!
I'm all alone and in big trouble.

Psalm 25:16 (MSG)

Colleagues tell me that writing is a lonely life, so perhaps I should be accustomed to those empty times when a river of distance flows through the living room between Jerry and me. But I never feel less alone than when I'm writing. Perhaps because for me writing is a kind of prayer, so I am in a conversation. Or maybe all those characters living inside my head and trying to get onto paper keep me from experiencing the depths of sadness that is a cousin to loneliness.

Any passions—painting, gardening, working with wood, photography, quilting, reading—can take us to places where loneliness is sewn into a pocket that we may carry with us but that for the moment is contained.

For someone who cares for another, whose daily duties take on the mundane, finding ways to feel less lonely is essential. Prayer, yes. A time of meditation, a centering prayer, can remind me that God has turned toward me. Allowing myself permission to take time for those passions that keep loneliness at bay involves believing that I am worth it. That may be the hardest task—believing I am worth the time to put loneliness where it belongs. Away.

God sets the lonely in families.

Psalm 68:6

The word *family* comes from the Latin word *famulus*, meaning "servant." When I first read this, I remember sitting back in my chair, surprised. We live in an era where families often work hard to meet the needs of children, to work two jobs (if possible), to ensure that children receive the best of everything so they are ready to tame the world as they step out into that arena. But family as servant lends a different tint to the picture.

Having a servant's heart serves others and is a healthy action for ourselves. When illness strikes, new people become our family. Occupational therapists, home care nurses, physical therapists. The office staff of cardiologists and neurologists and the rehab center, the techs administering radiology or chemo become people more familiar with my husband's daily challenges than extended family informed now and then by phone.

For me, the caregiver support group is a new family. It proves to be a place of respite and laughter, and offers a family who shares the elusive shadows that come and go, which we describe as shades of loneliness. It took me time to join the group, but within it is a community of faith where I have friends who understand, who share their challenges being a servant within their families. They serve as a prayer where I may be silent but not alone.

*But yield unselfishly to others and constantly
manifest a forgiving spirit towards all men.*

Titus 3:2 (WEY)

This sounds so noble—yet impossible to perfect. Especially on days when I'm annoyed that my husband may have enough energy to have coffee with his pals but not enough energy to unload the dishwasher. Stepping back, yielding unselfishly to others becomes an ending to a song I do not know the words to.

After the annoyance, I drove to town and had to pause before the yield sign. It has another meaning besides letting go, letting others move on through before me. It also means harvest, what we bring in at the end of the season.

Today, that's what I'll remember when I feel annoyance burning in my belly like bad jalapeño peppers. What yield do I want from this difficult time? I'd like the peace of a servant's heart, someone able to manifest a forgiving spirit, and one who seeks the harvest of a marriage that sings through sickness and in health.

I'll have to yield that harvest to "him who gives me strength."

*You were taught, with regard to your former
way of life, to put off your old self, which
is being corrupted by its deceitful desires; to
be made new in the attitude of your minds;
and to put on the new self, created to be like
God in true righteousness and holiness.*

Ephesians 4:22-24

Y is the first letter in *yield*. Today, for me, *y* stands for *Yahweh*, the only truly personal name of God. In Hebrew that name is connected to a verb that means "to be, to become." In my long years working in mental health, "being" without "doing" proved a resting point along life's journey, where judging lives by productivity takes a backseat to lives that are valued just because they exist.

I've begun to think during this time of caring for another that we are all, all the time, coming into being. While I don't think of the challenges and changes being gifts of new creations, they are. We laugh at the cat kneading the dog's back with his paws and how the dog actually seems to like it. Who would have thought?

We are finding joy in the midst of preparing medications for the day by being present in that moment. We are being, creating a moment and memory we can later draw on when we might otherwise feel irritable or sad. We've changed our eating habits, paying more attention to nutrition, which is good as we come "to be" healthier, and one of us comments on the change as being good. We speak differently about ways to show affection to each other, actually say the words "Could you hold my hand?" instead of merely wishing the other would know what would make us happier. Created in God's image, Yahweh's image, we come into being.

Each day is a new creation, and Yahweh is the cornerstone of the construction. What new creation will I work on today? Making room to be, not worry about doing, if only for five minutes, thanking Yahweh for the privilege.

"Take heart, daughter," he said,
"your faith has healed you."

Matthew 9:22

I'm still working on yielding. The second letter in *yield* is *i*. While it could well stand alone—and often does—I prefer to have that letter be a part of yield as it brings to mind an old medical term from the early nineteenth century. The word is *incarn* and it means "to grow new flesh."

After Jerry's fall, he had three dollar-bill-size patches of lost skin on his arm. We tended it, put medication on it, and then wrapped it and iced it, waiting for new flesh to grow. It's said that our skin is the largest organ in our body, and it works daily to replace itself. When there's trauma, then the skin must work double time.

Growing new flesh is what we have to do each day when we're looking after someone else. Frustrations happen. Wounds of words can take extra time and much energy to heal.

Word wounds are not unique to caregivers and their loved ones. I've had to grow new flesh at committee meetings or when reading unflattering book reviews. It's a part of the growth of who I am, and yielding to healing rather than holding on to hurt promises energy for more important things like laughing and loving.

I'm pretty certain I can't grow that new flesh alone… and yielding to that truth brings me closer to the presence of the Holy Spirit.

*I can do all this through him
who gives me strength.*

Philippians 4:13

hen there is the letter *e* in *yield*. In Latin, the prefix *en-* means "to be at one with" whatever word
that follows. *Enlighten* means to be at one with light.
Encourage means to be at one with courage.

It takes courage to be on the journey of yielding.
We're taught to be strong, to stand firm. We're told that
giving in or yielding is a sign of weakness, lack of mission
or desire, maybe even lack of principle. Yet Poet Laureate
William Stafford once noted that when struggling and
falling down, one should "lower the standard." At times
we should bring down the flag that snaps toward victory,
a victory that might not come until we pull back and yield.

To yield in the daily care of another requires courage
and encouragement. Jerry corrects what he thinks is an
error in my words, an error that has little meaning, really,
maybe the name of a hotel where we once stayed. I want to
"correct" back, but I know that if I do, I'll escalate an argu-
ment of little consequence. So I yield to his perception of
reality this day. I'm sure there are days he yields to mine.

Known to be stubborn and strong willed (the other
side of perseverance and resilience), I gather encouragement from the words "I can do all this through him who
gives me strength," including yielding to another yet one
more time. While waiting, yielding, I'll find both *enlight-
enment* and *encouragement* and, I hope, pass it on.

"I was sick and you looked after me."

Matthew 25:36

Before pulling into traffic at the yield sign, I look to my left to make sure it's the right time to merge into the flow, waiting patiently (usually) before accelerating. My mind can't wander about what to have for dinner or whether I left the curling iron plugged in. I must focus on the task at hand or I will soon hear the horns of cars behind me bringing me back to this moment. I must *look* and then proceed.

When Jesus said that He was sick and His friends *looked* after Him, I am reminded that the simple act of being aware, staying in the moment with a friend, a loved one, not letting my mind wander to what I'll say in response to whatever they are saying, is looking after them. It's yielding to their needs.

What a gift it is to yield my worries about saying just the right thing and instead to give full attention to the other person in my world. If there is a reward on this earth for such looking, it is the words of someone saying, "Thank you for listening. You didn't tell me what to do, you simply let me look at things, and that helps me find my own way."

Today I resolve to look and listen without merging into my day before I've truly paid attention.

*He anointed us, set his seal of ownership
on us, and put his Spirit in our hearts as a
deposit, guaranteeing what is to come.*

2 Corinthians 1:22

In 2009, pilot Sully Sullenberger became a hero by landing his damaged plane safely in the Hudson River on a cold January day. All passengers and crew survived. Later, in a television interview, he said that every landing he'd made in his career was a deposit for one huge withdrawal on that January day.

His words reminded me that each time I yield to another's needs, I am making a *deposit* that I can draw against on those days when I feel I've failed miserably in this task of giving to others. I'd like to say it is a privilege to serve, but that understanding comes in hindsight. I felt it a privilege *after* my sister moved on to more life, but during my time of caring for her, I found myself wanting to go on a long vacation away from her varying needs. One day she wanted me to negotiate with estranged family members; another day she ran an ad to run a new business from her hospital bed in the middle of the living room. Caring for her then did not feel like privilege.

But later, to know that I had made deposits of giving, that I had done my best to demonstrate God's love when I rubbed her feet until she was comforted enough to sleep or held her in the shower with warm water washing over us, cleansing away not only the dirt of daily living but of past hurts or disappointments that had little meaning at these end times of her life.

I yielded to her needs. Those deposits made years ago I draw on now, to give to another just as God put His Spirit in all our hearts "guaranteeing what is to come."

*I rejoice greatly in the Lord that at last
you renewed your concern for me…I
am not saying this because I am in
need, for I have learned to be content
whatever the circumstances.*

Philippians 4:10-11

The real problem is that I'm not by nature a caregiver. I know people who are. My friend Carol notices the little things to make her husband's days with health concerns go more easily. She cuts his hair. She bakes him pies. Another friend makes sure the right thickness of pillow lies behind his loved one's head. Another never runs out of her mother's favorite food.

These caregivers know just the right thing to say to ease another's discomfort or to make them laugh. Me? I have to pull myself from my internal musings to notice, to pay attention. At times my empathy meter doesn't even rise to one on a scale of ten. This concerns me, but then again, such concern makes it all about me and a good caregiver is about "the other."

Paul in his letter to the Philippians appears to understand that we are all different and able to give in different ways, at different times. He spends no time lamenting what his friends have not done for him but in praising what they have given. "Whatever is true, whatever is noble, whatever is right, whatever is pure, whatever is lovely, whatever is admirable…think about such things… And the God of peace will be with you."

Today I will think on the caregiving that my heart and hands have given rather than on what I lack. Just for a moment I won't compare myself to my friend Carol. Instead, I'll thank God that even though I don't drink milk, I remembered to buy it for Jerry yesterday before he ran out.

Trust in the LORD with all your heart
and lean not on your own understanding.

Proverbs 3:5

I t's the uncertainty I chew on without the satisfaction
of a swallow. Why a heart attack and stroke when
my husband stayed so active, ate well, took good care of
himself? How much exercise can he do now without risk
of further damage? Was his fall down ten steps brought
on by some small stroke or simply because he missed the
step as any of us might? How can I prevent more trouble
for his already battered body?

I try to remember that living with uncertainty is chis-
eling my character, allowing the sculpture of my life to be
polished by faith in ways it would otherwise never be. Our
years on the homestead were rife with challenges, from
burying a phone line seven miles (twice) to surviving an
airplane accident to taking on a granddaughter for a time
while her parents organized their lives. We not only survived those challenges but discovered strengths we didn't
know we had. We had no answers for the disappointments but came to look later for the lessons.

What I've come to hope is that there will be answers
one day. Until then, I will trust the Lord, if only for a
moment at a time, and learn to lean on someone larger
than myself.

But may the righteous be glad
and rejoice before God;
may they be happy and joyful.

Psalm 68:3

know my husband is doing better because his old obstinacy is back. All right, maybe mine is back too. But after his stroke and heart attack, he deferred to me in all questions. He accepted what I said about memories past, never once interrupted my storytelling as he was wont to do before. It was his nature to offer an alternative to whatever I might suggest, not as a sign that what I offered was inadequate (though that's how I often took it), but because he's an idea guy, coming up with options, ways to fix things.

After the stroke, I longed for an opinion even if it differed from mine. A little resistance would have been pleasant; a tiny disagreement, even a stated preference for what he might want to eat, would have been welcome. He was always adamant about beef over fish.

Now that he's being more of his former self, I'm given the "opportunity" to step over the annoyance of his corrections in my memory, to sigh quietly when he wants venison stroganoff when I'd prefer that tuna salad. Instead of being annoyed at his passiveness, now I'm complaining about his assertiveness.

I'm always telling my writing students that we can change how we feel and we do it all the time. When my husband was deep in the throes of healing, I missed his old vigor; now that his vigor is back, I long for a little placidness. But both behaviors are of him and make him who he is, the one I love, and that's what I hold on to.

Even on days when I try to live with what isn't so, I can make the choice to be happy rather than being right—if only for today.

The Lord is in his holy temple;
let all the earth be silent before him.

Habakkuk 2:20

With all the demands—doctor appointment changes, new health concerns, family consternations, financial valleys, work obligations, community commitments, the list is endless—where is wisdom to be found?

An old Jewish proverb says, "Silence is the fence around wisdom."

Today I will make time for silence. Contemplative prayer asks only that we sit quietly, palms open to receive, sometimes repeating a word given in prayer to bring focus back to silence so that we might embrace the love God so longs to shower upon us. My word is *heart,* chosen long before Jerry's heart attack and stroke. I return to it when I find my mind wandering onto the day's events rather than staying within the silence.

Mother Teresa wrote, "Souls of prayer are souls of great silence." How I need this! How I need the fence around wisdom that I might capture it during these times of confusion and need.

Give me today the wisdom to seek Your presence in the silence.

This is the day that the LORD has made;
let us rejoice and be glad in it.

Psalm 118:24 (NRSV)

h, right—don't worry, be happy.

Sometimes Scripture seems so far from my reality I wonder who those people were who wrote down words of praise and joy! Were they ever the parent of a chronically ill child or the spouse of a terminally ill soul or the daughter or son of a mother or father who no longer remembers who they are—or perhaps all three of those at once?

Though we are not told who wrote this psalm, the psalm itself reveals some of the story of the author of those cheering words. He had challenges much greater than mine today. And I am buoyed by his story that if he can endure great hardships and still be ready to praise the day that the Lord has made, if he can rejoice, then I can too, if only for a moment.

I can find a thread of praise to weave into my cape of woe, perhaps even tear out those old threads of self-pity and knit into it instead rejoicing and gladness. I will get out my knitting needles now before I change how I feel.

"For I know the plans I have for
you," declares the LORD, "plans to
prosper you and not to harm you, plans
to give you hope and a future."

Jeremiah 29:11

I once had a character in a book say, "Dreams are formed of fragments of hope, life and faith make the rest." It was a story based on a woman who longed to make a difference in the lives of those around her and who also found herself caring for an ill husband.

Funny how sometimes fiction features life. As Jerry and I have moved through many chapters of his illnesses in our marriage, we've met some of those diagnoses with hope. A torn colon that required him to be air-lifted from the ranch, for example, had us praying the doctor's hands would be swift and sure and that we'd caught the danger in time. His cancer brought a different kind of hope after complications of treatment left him with tuberculosis. How far he'd recover from his stroke and heart attack left us with fragments of hope. Life and faith made the rest. And none of this addressed his many crushed vertebrae resulting from an industrial accident in the 1970s.

At times we wondered if this was the best it would be and it was all downhill from there. Our challenge became how to find new dreams and hopes even within that fragile reality.

Jeremiah gave us courage to seek those new dreams.

The same God who had plans for the nation of Israel, though her situation at the time was dire, has plans for us as well, and they are to give us a future and a hope.

For those whose loved one is drifting from them with dementia or Alzheimer's, the hope may be in having strength and wisdom to give their days safety, warmth, and love. It might be the hope that at last other family members will recognize their relative's limitations and honor the caregiver who so often toils alone. Maybe it's discovering new activities both can share and look forward to that in another time would have seemed too tame for mutual joy.

I trust there is a plan...and it is not to bring me harm but to give me hope. And perhaps with faith to form another dream to take us forward into this next unknown.

*Let your eyes look straight ahead; fix your
gaze directly before you…Do not turn to the
right or the left; keep your foot from evil.*

Proverbs 4:25,27

Some years ago I took a class that included a night walk. With flashlights beaming right and left, we exited the classroom and walked to a forested area not far away. The goal was to notice what was in front of us, to ponder just what we could see before us in the shaft of bouncing light. Before long, my classmates' voices drifted in different directions. The small group I was with had broken up as people stayed longer in one place while others moved on around them. Before long, I was alone.

Anxiety crept up the back of my neck. I had planned to stay with the crowd, not get too far ahead nor lag behind. But somehow in my pausing to ponder the path at my feet, I'd set my own course, separate from the others, and now I was alone.

That is the way of caregiving too. We are alone though we may welcome support from others, find respite from time to time with the kindness of family and friends. Still, we started on a path that took a twist, and now all we can see ahead is what is at our feet with a small beam of light to guide us. But that can be enough, that little globe of illumination. And there can be a smidgeon of confidence in knowing that while we are separated from the crowd for a time, we can still make our way undaunted.

I returned to the classroom that evening by simply following the path at my feet, trusting in the Light to guide me and gaining strength from the accomplishment.

Aaron and Hur held [Moses's] hands up—
one on one side, one on the other—so that
his hands remained steady till sunset.

Exodus 17:12

Sometimes I speak at schools and tell the children stories of the way things used to be. I show them a burden basket carried by Native American women who put
only essential things inside the basket necessary for dig-
ging roots or bringing home nuts, berries, or fish. How
they placed the burdens in the basket helped them carry
their load. I often ask the children if they have burden bas-
kets, and they shout out "Our backpacks!" Those packs
have little zippered pockets meant to place the load so all
the items don't end up at the bottom of one pocket causing pain on their slender backs and shoulders.

How we carry our load makes such a difference in
how long we can endure the burden. Making sure we have
time away from our caregiver role or find respite from our
seeking job interviews that don't come our way is one way
of shifting that load. Allowing others to see our burden is
not a sign of weakness but of courage.

When the Amalekites attacked the Israelites after
they had crossed the Red Sea, Moses, Aaron, and Hur
observed the battle from the top of a hill. As long as Moses
held up his hands, the Israelites were winning. When his
arms tired, his friends stood on either side of him to support him and steady his weary hands. Moses gave them a

gift when he let them; imagine the impact if he'd refused their help in managing that burden.

Today I'll keep in mind that burden basket and the strength it took for Moses to allow others to share the load. When someone says, "May I help?" I'll look for a way to make that so. They can walk the dog, pick up milk at the store, go by the post office to mail that package, come sit with Jerry for a time while I run errands. And I'll accept my friend's offer to go see a movie with her where we can laugh and renew a friendship often set aside during difficult times.

It's no small thing to let another help carry our burden.

The desert and the parched land will be glad;
the wilderness will rejoice and blossom.

Isaiah 35:1

Not being a gardener doesn't mean I don't appreciate the beauty of flowers and the insights about life that gardens bring. While researching about a Northwest garden, I stumbled across this bit of wisdom: What brings on the bloom is not the quality of the soil nor the tending nor fertilizing nor even putting a stake beside the plant before it looks to need it. All those may help. But what brings on the bloom is the increased exposure to the light, the lengthening of the days.

The metaphor for my relationship with God burst out at me! In my rushing through the days, focused on the tasks at hand in caring for another, being purposeful facing challenges and praying I am doing God's work in my life, I find myself neglecting to take in the light, to appreciate the increased exposure to what will bring about blooms.

As spring approaches and the lilacs promise colorful, scent-filled petals, as summer freshens the air with the hawthorn tree's vibrant pink and glorious aroma, as the peonies and hydrangea and wildflowers shower the grounds with color, I will remember to thank the master gardener who owned this home before us.

Even more, I will remember to thank the Creator, who brings us light with prayers that there is still time for me to bloom in this latest caregiving garden God's given me.

*Now faith is confidence in what we hope for
and assurance about what we do not see.*

Hebrews 11:1

The first president of the Czech Republic, Václav Havel, wrote of hope, saying it was an orientation of the spirit, an orientation of the heart. He said it was the ability to begin something not just because it might succeed but because it was a good thing to do. All might not turn out well, but some things were worth doing "regardless of how they turn out."

My friend brought her mother into her home in her declining years. She hoped she might give to her in ways she had not been able to when my friend had married and left home at an early age, leaving her mother behind. She had faith that these later years of her mother's life could be a time of hope in a changed relationship. And it was so.

When my older sister was diagnosed with a rare but fatal multisystem disorder, I hoped we might find a truce in our difficult relationship. I wasn't her primary caregiver...there were others with more generous hearts than mine to change her sheets, fill her feeding tube, and help her in the night. I was a weekend warrior, paying her bills, negotiating thorny issues with an estranged husband, giving caregivers respite. But I had faith that my time with my sister would bring renewal. And it was so.

Once while I put lotion on her slender limbs, she said, "Thank you for being here through all this." She was spare with compliments, so I remember looking up at her to see if I'd really heard her correctly. "I couldn't have done it without you."

"Maybe it's only how involved and scary this all is that I showed up."

"No," she said. "You were always there for me. I just didn't notice."

Living by faith doesn't mean there will be no trials; it means we have someone in the wilderness places of our lives loving us just as we are, paying attention. My sister's words help me now to notice, to pay attention to the things not seen, and to allow what I hope for to renew my faith.

God is always here. Help me to notice.

*"You will seek me and find me when
you seek me with all your heart."*

Jeremiah 29:13

have become my husband's Google. This is not a
role I relish. He asks, "When did…Who invented…
Do you know where I put…?" These are dreaded words
within our marriage. It's not that I'm more organized than
he is, I'm not. I have collection problems too.

(I call them collections since watching a special on
hoarders. Collectors are further up on the food chain, or
so I'm hoping. The program was enough to make me dive
into a closet, tossing things out, hoping I can keep *hoarder*
as a word to describe "list of words I love" rather than as a
mental disorder I might be denying.)

With the challenges we're facing, we need to be more
organized to keep appointments, not waste hours wondering where we've stored that list of medications or the
insurance claim forms. Whenever one of us expresses frustration with a lost "collection" item, it is time to put seeking first—but seeking ways to support each other, ways
to seek God's will for our lives that we might draw closer
to Him in this time of trial. Then together we might find
what we're missing.

Today, I seek God as my better Google and the calm
God promises.

"Give, and it will be given to you. A good measure, pressed down, shaken together and running over, will be poured into your lap."

Luke 6:38

iving away is the yeast of life: it always rises more than expected and gives us more than imagined. Giving is one of the greatest ways we have of displacing sadness and hopelessness.

It's said that many great thinkers and doers of history suffered from depression and sadness. Martin Luther supposedly kept a list of things to do when he was *not* depressed. At the top of the list was "Do something for someone else."

Dorothea Dix, a mental health reformer from the early nineteenth century, endured a difficult childhood. She suffered emotionally and physically for many years, and yet crusaded on behalf of the mentally ill and brought relief to thousands. She discovered that relieving the suffering of others helped relieve her own.

As difficult as it is some days to feel confined and constrained by another's needs, to see a future darker than desired while hoping that light will pierce through if I persevere, I am lifted by the idea of giving, of the promise of things to come that I cannot yet see.

*"Seek first his kingdom and his righteousness,
and all these things will be given to you as well."*

Matthew 6:33

Perhaps more than anything, this time of chaos and caregiving makes me feel addled. I'm usually more focused, able to set goals and accomplish them, but of late, life intervenes. The residue left behind adds to my sense of scattered.

While researching a story, I had reason to look up the word *focus*. I wondered if it meant "clarity," the way we use the word today when we talk about taking a photograph and getting everyone in focus. Turns out it's a very old word, and it didn't originally mean clarity at all. It's from a Latin word that meant *hearth*, as in "the center of the home."

I love that. The hearth was where food was served. People shared the stories of their days there. Nurture was given and received, and the hearth was where the heat was. The farther from the source of heat one moved, the colder they became.

While I cannot control events that each day require my care in ways I had not planned, I can stay focused. I can decide what matters and where the center of my home is.

Jesus said that if we seek the kingdom of God—our hearth—then all things will be added. I may not get the laundry done as planned since there's a new doctor's appointment to be made. But as long as the hearth of my heart is clear, I will secure the promise of hope.

About Jane Kirkpatrick

A Wisconsin native and long-time Oregon resident, Jane's writing career began with "wretched little poems" as a child and progressed to nineteen novels and four nonfiction titles. Her first novel, *A Sweetness to the Soul,* earned the national Wrangler Award from the Western Heritage Center and was named to Oregon's One Hundred, celebrating the 100 best books about Oregon published in the previous 200 years. Several of her titles have been Oregon Book Award finalists, WILLA Literary Award winners, Christy finalists, and *New York Times* and national bestsellers.

Jane is a frequent retreat leader, keynote speaker, and presenter for a wide range of groups. Her writing career parallels her work as a mental health professional and clinical social worker, including working with families of children with disabilities on the Warm Springs Indian Reservation.

After more than a quarter century building and living on a remote homestead, with its share of difficult times, Jane and her husband, Jerry, returned to Bend, Oregon, in 2010 where she continues to write stories based on the lives of historical women or events and where she spoils her two dogs.

Jane can be reached at **www.facebook.com/theauthor janekirkpatrick**. Readers may also sign up for her monthly newsletter, *Story Sparks,* at **www.jkbooks.com** and contact Jane directly at that website.